WETLAND BIRDS

of North America

WETLAND BIRDS

of North America

A Guide to Observation,
Understanding and Conservation

Scott Leslie

KEY PORTER BOOKS

Library and Archives Canada Cataloguing in Publication

Leslie, Scott, 1963 –
    Wetland birds of North America : a guide to observation, understanding and conservation / Scott Leslie.

Includes bibliographical references and index.
ISBN 1-55263-722-0

    1. Water birds—North America—Identification. 2. Bird watching—North America—Guidebooks. I. Title.

QL681.L47 2006   598'.176'097   C2005-906161-8

ONTARIO ARTS COUNCIL
CONSEIL DES ARTS DE L'ONTARIO

The publisher gratefully acknowledges the support of the Canada Council for the Arts and the Ontario Arts Council for its publishing program. We acknowledge the support of the Government of Ontario through the Ontario Media Development Corporation's Ontario Book Initiative.

We acknowledge the financial support of the Government of Canada through the Book Publishing Industry Development Program (BPIDP) for our publishing activities.

Conservation status maps courtesy of NatureServe. 2004. NatureServe Explorer: An online encyclopedia of life [web application]. Version 4.1. NatureServe, Arlington, Virginia. Available at www.natureserve.org/explorer.

Range maps courtesy of Ridgely, R.S., T.F. Allnutt, T. Brooks, D.K. McNicol, D.W. Mehlman, B.E. Young, and J.R. Zook. 2003. Digital Distribution Maps of the Birds of the Western Hemisphere, version 1.0. NatureServe, Arlington, Virginia, USA.

NatureServe

Key Porter Books Limited
Six Adelaide Street East, Tenth Floor
Toronto, Ontario
Canada M5C 1H6

www.keyporter.com

Text design and formatting: Marijke Friesen
Photographs on pages 11 and 19: Paula Leslie

Printed and bound in China

06 07 08 09 6 5 4 3 2 1

For Paula, whose love, support and wisdom
have made so many things possible.

TABLE OF

CONTENTS

FOREWORD

Of the Earth's wild creatures, birds are the ones we have the most contact with. Unlike mammals, which tend to be shy and retiring, and are generally nocturnal or active at twilight, most birds are out and about during daylight hours. As the naturalist David Attenborough says, "They are lively; they are lovely; they are everywhere." They are present in our daily lives. The same is true of wetlands.

Many cities and towns that are found along lakeshores, seacoasts and rivers are adjacent to what remains of natural wetlands. In fact, millions of North Americans pass by wetlands on their daily commute, many of them unaware of the stunning wealth of life right under their noses. Such proximity and visibility is why both wetlands and birds are vital reminders of a parallel world made up of animals, plants and habitats, completely independent of our human existence.

Despite disappearing from the continent at a rate of about 150 acres every hour, gobbled up by urban development, agriculture, roads and the like, many wetlands hang on, providing homes for hundreds of millions of birds and other organisms across North America. Some are close at hand and accessible, others are remote. They are truly amazing places to visit and to know; they are the richest ecosystems on the continent, seething with life, brimming with beauty and complex beyond comprehension. Our lives are enhanced by the existence of wetlands as they, among other things, supply and purify our drinking water, regulate flooding and buffer against coastal erosion.

I hope this book succeeds in illustrating some of the wonderful diversity of wetland birds while helping you identify and understand them a little better. As well, it is my sincere wish that it conveys the need to protect their habitats. But I suppose my ultimate aim is to inspire you to visit a local wetland and see for yourself just how fascinating this important part of natural world is.

WONDERFUL WETLAND BIRDS

The Marsh is an entire world unto itself on the world of earth—a different world, which has its own life, its settled inhabitants and its passing travellers, its voices, it noises, and above all its mystery.

GUY DE MAUPASSANT

Concealed in my floating photographic blind, I watch a northern harrier as it glides over the marsh, sending flocks of startled water-birds into the golden evening light. Black ducks, mallards, teals, shovelers and ring-necks explode from the water, shattering its glassy surface. The air is filled with raucous quacking and the whistle of wings. A dozen greater yellowlegs, known also as tattlers due of their habit of "telling all" when in the presence of danger, take wing and announce with shrill alarm calls the harrier's arrival. The marsh is in complete upheaval.

The young hawk's flight is buoyant as she alternately flaps and glides away into the far reaches of the marsh. The ducks continue to orbit, finally settling to Earth once the harrier disappears from view. In the aftermath, duck-down feathers, dislodged during the fear-driven flurry of wings, sift back to earth like snowflakes.

Moments later the harrier re-appears, prompting

People enjoying a wetland, an accessible natural habitat rich in wildlife

more ducks to take flight and beginning the drama once more. Flying toward me over the shallow flats of the marsh, she frightens sandpipers, plovers and dowitchers from the mudflats into the air. In a chorus of peeps and weets they fly in tight zigzagging flocks in a successful effort to evade the hungry hawk. Like millions of others across the continent, these shorebirds have stopped over here during southern migration to refuel before continuing their long and difficult flight to the south.

Wetlands can explode with bird activity, such as these black ducks and green-winged teals taking flight

The harrier draws near. Ready for her arrival, I trip the shutter of my camera at just the right time, capturing a few frames in the perfect, soft light. She passes by me and continues to quarter the marsh without success until finally fading into the distance. Another drama comes to a close in this marsh, but countless similar events take place every day in thousands of wetlands across North America.

A stunning diversity of bird life inhabit the continent's wetlands. Here are just a few of them:

- The elegant sandhill crane, one of the continent's tallest and most marvelous birds.
- The male wood duck—considered by many to be the world's

most beautiful bird—in a royal adornment of green, blue and purple feathers, and ruby red eyes.

- The osprey, a large hawk nearly the size of an eagle. Displaying a mastery of both air and water, it dives with blazing speed from great heights, crashing into the water to catch fish in its massive talons.
- The Wilson's snipe, one of the most secretive and strangest birds with its extremely long bill and rear-set eyes.
- The majestic bald eagle, boldly plumed in dark brown and white, spiraling higher and higher into the sky for a better vantage point on potential prey.

There are plenty of interesting birds to be found in a wetland and, best of all, they're usually pretty easy to see. Marshes, ponds and lakes tend to be open areas and birds that inhabit them don't have the option of flying just a few yards and disappearing into the heavy cover of trees. They are surrounded by drier areas, and in a sense, small isolated wetlands are like islands, so birds are reluctant to take flight and leave altogether, otherwise they may have to fly a considerable distance to find another "island." And, although many secretive species, such as grebes, soras and teals live here, such birds can't help but spend much of their time in the open and can be spotted with practice.

But there's more to wetland birds than meets the eye. They also produce some of the strangest sounds heard in nature. Anything from the ridiculous—a groaning, crooning pied-billed grebe—to the sublime—a song sparrow in full serenade—can be heard. Most bizarre, however, is the American bittern, a small heron that burps out one of the strangest sounds in all of nature. The descriptive names given it sum it up well. Nineteenth-century writer and naturalist Henry David Thoreau variously called it "stake-driver," "pumper," "belcher-squelcher," "wollerkertoot," and "slug-toot." "It was a sound as of gulping water," he said. A picture might be worth a thousand words, but so is a name sometimes. Having heard it myself many times, I think it should be called the "Ga-LOOP-toot," but you really have to hear it to believe it.

What exactly is a wetland? Marshes, salt marshes, wooded swamps, shallow lake margins and ponds, fens, bogs, river margins, prairie potholes and sloughs are all considered wetlands. In the lower forty-eight states and Canada they cover approximately 700,000 square miles, approximately 10 percent of the total land area. Of the roughly 650 or so bird species that regularly breed north of Mexico, nearly one half use wetlands in some measure during their life cycles, and about one quarter are completely dependent on them. Of course we expect to see ducks and geese in

Diverse bird life abounds in the right wetland habitats, such as this group of herons, ibises and spoonbills

such habitats, but many other species not typically associated with wetlands are equally dependent on them. Among them are bald eagles, swallows and many species of small songbirds.

During the breeding season a wetland is alive and becomes a beehive of activity, hosting a concentration of bird life unmatched by any other habitat in North America.

At this time of year the most important events in birds' relatively brief lives occur: establishing territories, nest building, mating and rearing of young

Wetlands are unique environments where neither land nor water dominates. They harbor ideal conditions for producing a stunning array of living things from the smallest insect to the great blue heron. A myriad of aquatic and semiaquatic plants, such as bulrushes, spikerushes, cattails, reedgrasses, pond lilies and duck-weeds and other species take energy from the sun and convert it into food more efficiently than do plants in any almost other environment. Wetlands are, as the early twentieth-century naturalist Donald Peattie said, "Life, in short, synthesized, plant-synthesized, light synthesized." The diverse bird life thrives upon the abundant fruits of this marriage of chlorophyll and sunlight.

The photosynthesis of sunlight into plants, a process that runs at a particularly furious pace in many wetlands, results in an exuberance of life. The sun's intensity, growing with each passing spring day, fuels this most basic of all biological processes. The waters warm into late spring and early summer (a decidedly year-round process, however, in the most southerly regions of the continent). As a result, countless aquatic plants, from tiny single-celled algae to emergent cattails, are conjured into existence on little more than light, water, carbon dioxide and minerals. The key to such high productivity in wetlands is the shallow water's ability to absorb the sun's heat and maintain a relatively constant temperature that is ideal for rapid plant growth. Besides providing food directly for herbivorous birds such as ducks, microscopic animals and tiny insects also dine on this abundant vegetation, in turn feeding invertebrate-consuming birds, reptiles, amphibians, fish and dragonflies.

The productivity of wetlands has played a vital role in evolution through the eons and continues to be a hotbed of life. De Maupassant hit the nail on the head when he wrote, "For, was it not in stagnant and muddy water, amid the heavy humidity of

Certain wetland areas may not host large numbers of birds, but some, like this northern lake, are home to beautiful species, such as this common loon

moist land under the heat of the sun, that the first germ of life pulsated and expanded to the day?"

Since I do much of my fieldwork concealed in a small floating blind, I'm literally immersed in the habitat, approaching wildlife on its own terms, close up, at eye-level. This requires slow approaches (sometimes many hours), long waits, hungry mosquitoes and thirst.

(When working in the blind I don't dare drink anything because yet another urge of nature might call, interrupting and ruining a long, stealthy approach!) There's also the discomfort of lying prone on a small platform for the better part of a day in the summer heat or the cold of early spring. And, of course, after all that work, I might come up empty-handed. But it is all worth being able to observe and photograph, very close at hand, the private lives of diverse creatures that would normally flee at the barest hint of human presence.

Some species, such as this red-winged blackbird can be seen in practically any kind of wetland anywhere on the continent

It is my hope that the photographs and text that follows will inspire the reader to a greater curiosity and interest in wetland birds and the complex and fertile ecosystems they call home and, in doing so, help raise awareness of the critical need to protect them.

A note about the species included in this book: With literally several hundreds of different species of birds using wetland environments at some point in their lives, it would be almost impossible to cover all of them in a book of this format, it would simply be too large. The species presented in this book are a representative selection of "core" birds found throughout North American wetlands.

WETLANDS: A DIVERSITY OF HOMES FOR BIRDS

It is difficult to convey the sheer number of birds on the beach here to someone who has not seen it. There are literally tens of thousands of semi-palmated sandpipers competing for limited space as the incoming tide narrows the beach with each passing minute. I decided the best way to deal with this challenge was to allow them to come to me so I could photograph them at close range. I watched an earlier high tide to see where the birds congregate on the beach. Then, with the tide still well out (and the birds still busy feeding on the mudflats) I positioned myself in a good spot and waited. Eventually the birds drew closer in advance of the rising tide. I remained as still as possible. After about 1½ hours, I was literally engulfed by thousands of peeping sandpipers as I lay flat on my stomach with my camera resting on a low support in front of me. The birds were bumping into me left and right, and huge flocks took off and landed in perfect unison around me. Of course, I would soon have to retreat in advance of the tide, too.

On the Upper Bay of Fundy between the provinces of New Brunswick and Nova Scotia, hundreds of thousands or perhaps millions of semi-palmated sandpipers stop over during their southward migration each summer to feed on the abundant mud-shrimp found in the extensive mudflats. Single flocks of up to a quarter of a million birds have been reported. I try to imagine the awesome sight of such a mass of birds on the wing, twisting and turning in perfect unison, a living cloud blotting out the sun! By some estimates, most of the continent's entire population of the semi-palmated sandpipers depend on these rich feeding grounds.

These semi-palmated sandpipers take advantage of the food available on an Upper Bay of Fundy tidal mudflat wetland

Semi-palmated sandpiper migration in the Bay of Fundy is just one example of the many bird spectacles that occur in wetlands across North America. Hundreds of thousands of sandhill cranes descend on Nebraska's Platte River during migration every spring. (The surrounding area, known as The Sandhills, is the bird's namesake.) Delaware Bay supports up to a million migrating shorebirds each spring, including 80 percent of the eastern population of red knots. Other places such as Last Mountain Lake in Saskatchewan, for example, are vital migratory stopovers for a wide variety of wetland birds such as geese, ducks, shorebirds, cranes and birds of prey. Because of the sheer numbers of birds that rely on only 10 percent of North America's land base, it's not surprising that certain strategic wetlands host such great numbers of birds. However, for every remarkable hot spot like those above, there are thousands of small, apparently unremarkable wetland habitats that are vital to tens and perhaps hundreds of millions of North American birds.

Wetlands include many types of habitat, but one thing they all have in common is that birds use them all, to varying degrees, for nesting, breeding, feeding, drinking water and as important rest areas during migration. The type of wetland will determine, in large measure, what species of birds will be found there, but most wetland birds will be found at various times in any wetland type.

MARSHES

Freshwater marshes (sometimes they can also be brackish or alkaline) are what we tend to think of as wetlands. They are the most widespread and prevalent wetland environments on the continent. Marshes are special places where life pulses quickly. Here, in the realm of the cattail, the muskrat and the spring peeper, is one of the richest bird environments anywhere. The biological productivity of freshwater marshes rivals that of tropical rain forests. As a result, they sustain a biodiversity significantly out of proportion to their size.

Salt marshes, such as this one in the southern United States, provide a crucial wintering habitat for millions of wetland birds

Occurring along slow-moving streams, in the shallow margins of rivers, lakes and ponds, freshwater marshes are often contiguous with other bodies of water. What distinguishes them is their relatively permanent shallow water, from a few inches to 3 feet or deeper and the presence of emergent vegetation such as cattails, rushes and reeds.

Humans are creating more and more artificial marshes for waterfowl by building impoundments to catch and hold water. After some time, these newly made environments also happen to make good habitat for a whole host of other wetland species such as red-winged blackbirds, ducks, rails, herons and grebes, to name a few.

WET MEADOWS

Wet meadows are a type of freshwater marsh that forms in poorly drained, low-lying areas. During the summer breeding season, they usually have no standing water, but remain rather damp, soggy places in which water-loving vegetation such as sedges, rushes and certain grasses thrive in rich, fertile soil. Snipes, yellowlegs, northern harriers and soras are some of the species found nesting or foraging there.

PRAIRIE POTHOLES

Although they account for only about 10 percent of the total wetland area in North America, prairie potholes (also know as sloughs) produce about 50 percent of the continent's waterfowl, especially mallards, wigeons, teals, shovelers, ring-necks and a host of other dabbling ducks. These wetlands, found exclusively in the upper Midwest of the United States and Canada's prairie provinces, were formed as the glaciers retreated, leaving millions of shallow depressions or "potholes" on the landscape that later filled with water.

TIDAL MARSHES

At one time, hundreds of miles of tidal marshes were found along the East Coast of North America from Canada's maritime provinces south through Florida and around the Gulf of Mexico. Today, most of them are gone, having been destroyed by settlements or coastal development. Pollution has also played a large part in reducing the ability of these marshes to sustain diverse ecosystems. Despite this, they are crucial areas providing habitat for clams, young fish, crabs and an abundance of other invertebrates such as mud worms and shrimp that birds rely on. They remain an important place for both breeding and migrating birds. Breeding birds include, among others, northern harriers, clapper rails, red-winged black-

Freshwater cattail marshes, such as this one, are the most common wetland habitats in Canada and the northern United States

birds, grackles, black duck and blue-winged teals (particularly where there are salt ponds). Savannah sparrows nest in the upland areas adjacent to the salt-marsh, while song sparrows, common yellowthroat and yellow warblers are found in the bushy margins.

During spring, fall and winter, the tidal marshes are important resting and feeding areas for migrating herons, sandpipers, plovers, ducks and geese, among others. Some of them may spend the entire winter here. Tidal marshes can be fresh, brackish or salt water. They can be located on exposed coastlines, in estuaries (very productive ecosystems that are created where a river meets the sea), or associated with beaches and barrier islands. One thing they have in common is that they are all, to one degree or another, affected by the ocean tides. For example, as the level of the tide changes in an estuary, birds' access to different food sources changes dramatically. Low tide favors smaller invertebrate-eating birds such as sandpipers and plovers, while high tide may favor the long-legged, fish-eating egrets and herons. Terns and ospreys may also take advantage of high tide to catch small fish in the deeper water.

SWAMPS

In North America, historically, swamps have been thought of as forbidding wastelands, no-man's lands where nothing good could be found. This unfortunate perception led to the wanton destruction of vast tracts of swampland over the past two centuries.

Swamps are permanently or occasionally flooded areas that are characterized by saturated soils and dominated by woody plants. They are often adjacent to rivers, lakes and other waterways. Plant commu-

Some wetlands, such as cypress swamps in the southern United States, are now quite uncommon, many of them having been destroyed by development

nities within swamps range from microscopic plankton to large dominant trees such as red maple in the U.S. Northeast and Canada, willow in the western part of the continent and bald cypress in the southeastern United States. They are important habitats for cavity-nesting waterbirds such as hooded and common mergansers, wood ducks, buffleheads and goldeneye ducks. Barred owls and red-shouldered hawks will often nest in swamps and, due to their frequent isolation, they are prime colony sites for herons, egrets, ibises, spoonbills and the endangered wood stork. It was thought that the ivory-billed woodpecker, a magnificent bird with a wingspan of over 3 feet, was driven to extinction by the destruction of swamp and bottomland forest in the southeastern United States over half a century ago. In April 2005 it was happily confirmed that the bird still exists in the "big woods" of eastern Arkansas.

Florida's coastal mangrove swamps, in addition to being an important habitat to a whole host of bird species, are critical nursery areas for marine reef fish and invertebrates.

BOGS AND POCOSINS

Bogs, more northerly habitats, are formed in low areas where rainwater and snowmelt accumulates. Found in the northeastern U.S.,

The near-shore shallows of this southern lake provide wetland habitat for a host of bird species

the Great Lakes region and much of Canada, they are one of the quintessential features of the North, playing an important role in the makeup of the great boreal forest. Because of decomposing sphagnum moss, which is the dominant plant, bogs are generally very acidic, making them less productive than many other wetlands, but they are important habitats nevertheless and provide homes for species such as soras, bitterns, ducks and nesting shorebirds.

Pocasins, the southern counterpart to bogs, are located from Virginia to Florida. These are poorly drained wooded and shrubby areas containing tree species such as pond pine, loblolly pine and sweet bay. Like bogs, they are not highly productive, but serve as important habitat to a number of bird species. The endangered red-cockaded woodpecker, the pileated woodpecker and common yellowthroat are a few of the bird species found in pocasins. Less than 1,400 square miles of pocasins remain.

FENS

Fens are similar in appearance to bogs, but derive their water from drainage, runoff and groundwater instead of exclusively from rainwater as bogs do. Less acidic than bogs, they are biologically more productive and host a diverse community of plant life, which typically includes grasses, sedges, rushes and wildflowers.

Fens are home to many familiar wetland birds. Bitterns, pied-billed grebes, various species of ducks and great blue herons, among other species, live in fens.

OTHER WETLAND TYPES

Playa lakes are temporary wetlands that form when shallow circular depressions in the ground are filled by rainwater. Some 25,000 playa lakes are found throughout the southern high plains of the United States. Because they form where there are few permanent water sources in areas that often receive 20 inches or less of rain per year, they are often the only wetland habitats for great distances. Playa lakes can host a stunning array of birdlife. Sandhill cranes, blue-winged teals, bald eagles and red-winged blackbirds are just a few of the species found at these ephemeral watery jewels.

Like playa lakes, woodland and vernal pools are temporary, seasonal wetlands. West Coast vernal pools are found from Oregon south to the Mexican border. Typically filled by winter rains, these shallow pools form in surface depressions and can remain flooded from weeks to months at a time. Because they are isolated from other more permanent aquatic areas, they are an important habitat

Temperate zone lakes and fens are key habitats for many species of wetland birds, but have been hit hard by acid rain, which can result in the depletion of vital fish populations

for many species of rare plants in particular. The high population of insects attracts insectivorous birds such as swallows and fly-catchers and the abundant frogs attract green herons.

Woodland vernal pools are wetlands that form after rainwater or snowmelt fills pockets on the forest floor. They are anywhere from a few square yards to pond size. Because they generally lack any fish that would act as predators, insects are able to reproduce freely, creating abundant food for the insectivorous birds that may use woodland pools such as the yellow-rumped warbler, the common yellowthroat and the alder flycatcher. These birds will often hunt by "hawking," where they make short flights from a perch to catch an insect.

WETLANDS: AN INTRICATE WEB OF LIFE

I look with keen anticipation through the gauze of oscillating mayflies to the cove beyond. It is covered with water lilies and brimming with life. A beaver dam has blocked the flow of the little brook that runs from the cove, flooding the area and transforming it into a marshy, languid pool.

As I emerge from the trees that edge the cove, a startled ring-necked duck patters across the pond before finally taking flight. Several painted turtles sunning themselves on a log plop into the water. It's surprising how acute the senses of these little turtles are—they contradict our usual stereotypes of reptiles. A wood duck hen and her train of young quietly glide by, unaware of my presence. Overhead, an osprey is on a keen lookout for fish for its hungry young, while on a tiny exposed bar at the edge of the cove, a loon carefully rearranges the eggs on her muddy nest.

Secret lives such as these are lived in this little wetland and thousands of others across North America. The best-kept secret of all, however, is just how complex a wetland ecosystem is. To truly appreciate its intricate nature, an

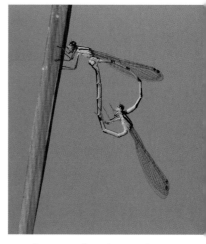

Insects, such as these mating damselflies, are a vital strand in the complex food web of a wetland

amphibious approach is needed. So, once I've surveyed the world above with its birds and damselflies, I don a mask and snorkel and slip under the cove's surface into the cool, softly lit water beneath.

Magical underwater groves of pond lilies spring from the muddy bottom a few feet below to stretch long, sinuous stems toward the surface, each topped by a single oval leaf that soaks up life-giving sunlight. In water tinted bronze by plant tannins, the light slants through the fragile grove, illuminating schools of golden shiners and minnows and a lone painted turtle swimming through the delicate understory. In deeper water, a large snapping turtle stirs as my shadow crosses its prehistoric eye, then nonchalantly swims away over the muddy bottom. Leeches, undulating ribbons of black and red flesh, ply the shallows in search of a host. Dragonflies dab the water above me, creating tiny concentric ripples as they pluck prey from the surface. A dark shape moves through the water in the distance, perhaps a pied-billed grebe diving for minnows.

Frogs are a key component of the freshwater wetland ecosystem, providing food for wading birds. Unfortunately, their populations are plummeting for various human-caused environmental reasons

In a wetland there really is no boundary separating the sunlit world of trees, birds and sky from the dim world of pond lilies, fish and mud. All organisms here are members of a food chain that connects a minnow about to be snapped up by a hungry perch to an osprey 100 feet overhead, ready to dive and capture that same perch, thus transforming predator into prey.

Ultimately everything in a wetland, including birds, is dependent for survival upon the primary producers. Microscopic algae, duck weed, pond lilies, reeds, cattails and countless other species of plants combine sunlight with the incredibly rich supply of nutrients found in the water and soil to create the most productive habitat in North America. Birds may be some of the most "charismatic" (to use a term popular with biologists to describe highly visible species) residents of wetlands, but they are also parts of the ecosystem, playing a role no more or no less vital than every other organism that lives there.

Evolution has crafted a jigsaw puzzle of enormous complexity in this environment, where birds fit perfectly in virtually every niche that is available to them. Each niche of a given bird is made up of layer upon layer of trophic (feeding) relationships populated by lower organisms that go all the way down to the most basic level of the algaes. To illustrate this point, consider the particular chain of events that must occur before a tree swallow can get a meal for its hungry chicks. The late spring sun warms the shallow, nutrient-rich water. Microscopic aquatic algae drink up the sunlight and bloom into profusion, tingeing the water a light green and providing food for newly hatched insects such as mosquito larvae. Some time later, millions of these little wrigglers eventually develop into clouds of mosquitoes, which in turn become prey for elegant civil-bluet damselflies that pluck them from the air. Gracefully swooping over the pond, with its mouth gaping wide, a tree swallow scoops hapless damselflies on the wing, then returns to feed them to hungry chicks in the nest. And this extremely simplified example

Muskrats, the most common and widespread mammals inhabiting North America's wetlands, are important to the health of the ecosystem as they collectively consume enormous amounts of plant matter, which are ultimately recycled back into the environment

Most wetlands are immensely productive ecosystems, and contain as much biomass below the water as above

represents just a fraction of the actual complexity of trophic relationships involved in sustaining just one bird in a wetland!

In reality, there are probably as many kinds of places to find food in a wetland as there are species that inhabit it. Roughly speaking, a wetland can be divided into six zones within which food resources are found: the water column where fish, leeches and aquatic insects live; the bottom where mollusks, insects, larvae and crustaceans live; the submerged plants that produce stems and on which amphibians, insects and mollusks cling; the surface where duckweed and algae grow; exposed plants that bear fruits, leaves and seeds; and the air where insects and birds fly. Each species of bird in a wetland will exploit one or more of these places according to how it has evolved—a bittern hunting frogs in the shallows, a teal gleaning duckweed from the surface, a grebe fishing for leeches in deeper water, for example. The interconnections between everything that lives, even in a small wetland pond, are incomprehensibly vast. But thanks to millions of years of adaptation through natural selection, the system works!

In addition to all of the biological interactions between birds and other species, there are complex relationships and balances between birds and the physical environment of the wetland itself. The influence of water levels, water temperature and pH, weather, the amount of cover and shelter available and the presence of predators all affect the lives of wetland birds.

The great majority of turtles worldwide depend on freshwater wetlands as habitat

For birds the most important physical feature of any wetland is the availability of water. Water cover might be permanent or seasonal (ponds, marshes, fens, bogs), during high tide (tidal marshes) or after a heavy rainfall (vernal pools, playa lakes). Even when the surface water disappears for a time, the soil may be saturated enough to support the aquatic plants, such as cattails, reeds and rushes, that many birds rely on for shelter and as cover.

Water conditions that may be sufficient for some birds might not be for others. For example, sora rails are able to survive in very small patches of extremely shallow or dried-out habitats (as well as other wetter and larger wetlands) that are just damp enough to support cattails and other moisture-loving plants. In such an environment they have a source of food (seeds), nest-building materials and enough cover from predators. In contrast, the pied-billed grebe, another small bird, can't survive in such places because it needs a relatively large flooded area to land and take off from and deeper water to dive in for its prey. An osprey requires deep water that it can safely dive into from a great height, while a dowitcher needs water shallow enough to wade through while it feeds by probing the mud with its long bill. Each species has a particular set of conditions (in this case water depth) that must be met before it can successfully inhabit a wetland.

Fortunately, most wetlands aren't exclusively moist or flooded, deep or shallow, but are a combination of conditions that are suitable for a variety of birds. For example, in salt marshes the water level changes daily, flooding on the incoming tide and draining on the ebb tide. Shorebirds will feed on mudflats for crustaceans and mollusks during low tide, while other species like cormorants or great blue herons will often wait for high tide before they begin to fish.

Other factors also determine how many bird species will be found in a wetland. Larger wetlands tend to be more heterogeneous with a wider range of water depths and a more varied distribution of vegetation. This can result in a "patchiness" that provides a greater choice of potential microhabitats resulting in a higher diversity of species. The species of birds found in a wetland will also depend on the kinds of plants present.

Water temperature has an impact on how abundant food will be for birds. Lower temperatures usually mean a slower growth rate for the primary producers in the wetland—the algae, duckweeds and other plants. If the water temperature is too low, algae won't grow as quickly, and as one of the foundations upon which everything else depends, the entire food chain right up to the top will be affected. In other words, it might be a little harder for that tree swallow to feed her young if the water is just a little colder! Warmer water temperatures, of course, will have the opposite effect, generally increasing the mass of vegetation available and the number of birds present.

It should come as no surprise that wetlands, with such a high concentration of birds, attract large numbers of predators. Like a moat around a castle, water is a buffer against incursions by many predators, preventing their access to eggs or young in the nest. But some are undeterred by water and prey heavily on birds, eggs and young. Raccoons, skunks, minks, snapping turtles, pickerel, largemouth bass, snakes and alligators all take their toll, especially on the eggs and chicks. During particularly dry breeding seasons, water levels decrease and greater access to previously unreachable areas may open up, allowing predators to take more birds. Breeding success may also be lower for birds that nest near outer edges of a wetland, where they are more easily reached. Fortunately, the heavy vegetation that is a feature of the breeding areas of most wetlands provides a way for most nesting birds to conceal their nests effectively, enabling breeding success.

In a wetland, or any complex ecosystem for that matter, everything is more or less dependent on everything else. Tugging at just one strand in this web of biological and physical interactions can cause one species or a group of them to be less successful and another to become more so. For example, in the case of global warming, in which hotter, drier weather results in lower water levels in wetlands, pied-billed grebe populations may decline significantly while soras may survive with relatively few difficulties, at least for a time. Eventually global warming will affect everything in our wetlands in some way, possibly resulting in catastrophic changes.

Different species of birds utilize wetlands in different ways throughout the year. Wetland-dependent birds, including many ducks, grebes, rails, herons, loons, cranes, cormorants, shorebirds, some songbirds and a few birds of prey, rely almost exclusively on this environment for nesting, food and shelter during the breeding season. They are also highly dependent on them during migration and for overwintering.

Many other birds rely on wetlands for at least part of the year for vital activities such as feeding, drinking water or shelter from bad weather. For example, yellow warblers, song sparrows, bobolinks and common grackles, among others, while not completely dependent on

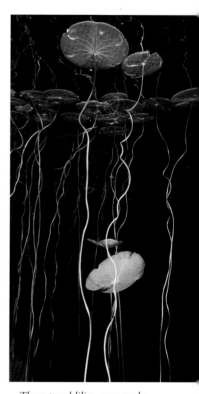

These pond lilies, seen underwater, are part of an aquatic ecosystem that is integral to the health of the whole habitat. There's often more than meets the eye in a wetland environment

them, nevertheless are commonly found about wetlands, tapping them for food and nesting materials. To varying degrees certain raptors also depend on wetland areas as a source of prey or, in the case of some, such as red-shouldered hawks, as a place to nest near.

All told, the number of bird species that require wetlands for their survival to some degree is estimated between one third and half of the roughly 650 species that regularly breed in North America, north of Mexico. The importance of protecting these vital habitats becomes clear when you consider that nearly half of our breeding birds, as well as countless other species, depend on a precious 700,000 square miles or 10 percent of the land area that is occupied by wetlands (not including Alaska). In fact, wetlands contain the greatest number of endangered, threatened and vulnerable species of any habitat in North America. In the United States approximately one half of all officially endangered species are dependent on wetlands, including seventeen species of birds. A similar situation exists in Canada.

The high proportion of endangered, threatened or vulnerable wildlife found in wetlands can be traced to two related facts. They are home to an inordinately large number of species in relation to their land area when compared with other North American habitats, and a greater percentage of wetlands have already been lost

A tree swallow completes the food cycle in a wetland by feeding its young some damselflies

(about half) compared to many other habitat types. Indeed, of the eight species of birds that have become extinct in North America in historical times (as recently as 1987 for the dusky seaside sparrow), five of them were birds that relied on wetlands. While various causes may have contributed to the extinction of the Eskimo curlew, Carolina parakeet, Bachman's warbler, dusky seaside sparrow and the Labrador duck (little is known of this bird's life history, but that it utilized tidal wetlands to some degree isn't far-fetched), the loss of a wetland habitat likely played at least some part in all of them.

Today, a real threat of extinction hangs over the heads of the majestic whooping crane, the Mississippi sandhill crane, the wood stork, the Everglades snail kite and the piping plover, to name just a few. All are officially endangered in North America and the loss of their wetland habitat is one of the primary reasons that they may disappear from this world forever. As well, geographical populations of many other species are in peril of extinction within limited ranges (a phenomenon called extirpation) in North America.

Despite being the most biologically productive ecosystems in North America, and providing a home to perhaps hundreds of millions of its avian residents, wetlands are being destroyed at a frightening rate. It is estimated that between 1780 and 1980 the conterminous U.S. lost over half or nearly 100 million acres of its original wetland habitats (most of Alaska's wetlands are still intact) and continues to lose about 110,000 acres annually. In Canada the numbers are no more encouraging. Estimates put the historical loss due to agricultural expansion alone at over 49 million acres. The losses continue. Over the past twenty years the world's focus has been on the destruction of tropical rain forests. North America's wetland ecosystems are like our tropical rain forests: They are the biological engines that drive avian (and much other) life on this continent. It is time we regard them in proportion to their importance.

INTRODUCTION TO THE SPECIES ACCOUNTS

It is not enough to know how to identify a bird. Just as important, and perhaps even more so, is an understanding of the way it lives. What habitats does it prefer? How does it feed and get around? What does it sound like? What does it eat? How does it nest and rear its young? Does it migrate and, if so, when? Who are its closest relatives? And perhaps the most important question of all, in light of the increasing pressure on the Earth's ecosystems by humans, how healthy is its population?

There are seventy-three species in this book, a selection of "core" wetlands species. Fifty-eight of them are included as "wetland-dependent species" in the American Ornithologists' Union's *Checklist of North American Birds*, 6th Edition, 1983, as referenced in "Wetlands as Bird Habitat" in the "National Water Summary on Wetlands Resources," U.S. Geological Survey Water-Supply Paper 2425, 1996, by Robert E. Stewart, Jr. The remaining thirteen species, though not included on the aforementioned list specifically, are cited in other publications as occurring in wetlands. These thirteen species feed in or near, nest in or near, or depend on wetlands during migration to such an extent that they would be considered de facto wetland birds (such as many shorebirds).

The species accounts are divided into seven main groupings, each one a chapter, i.e., Waterfowl, Wading Birds, etc. Each account features photographs of the bird as well as a natural history that is divided into nine sections. (Note: In the Family Life section of the species accounts, the number of eggs is the typical number incubated and does not include unusually large or small clutches.) The "Species status overall for North America" under the "Conservation Concerns" section for each species, as well as the range maps and conservation status maps are adapted from the NatureServe Explorer website (www.natureserve.org/explorer). Conservation status maps are included for those eighteen wetland species whose populations are most threatened. According to the map key, each map shows the level of threat in a given state or province where the bird occurs as a breeding species. A species may not need to be federally listed as endangered for it to be critically or otherwise imperiled within a state or province. A few of the maps may show a species as not existing in an area where in fact it does; this is a result of incomplete available data at the time of printing. NatureServe is a non-profit network of conservation data centres in Canada, the U.S. and Latin America that provide some of the most current and accurate data available to those working in the field of conservation biology.

RANGE MAP LEGEND

Permanent Resident	■	Breeding Resident	■
Nonbreeding Resident	■	Passage Migrant	□
Uncertain Status	▨	Introduced	■
Vagrant	■		

CONSERVATION MAP LEGEND

Presumed Extirpated	■	Possibly Extirpated	■
Critically Imperiled	■	Imperiled	■
Vulnerable	□	Apparently Secure	■
Secure	■	Not Ranked/ Under Review	▨

WATERFOWL

CANADA GOOSE

Branta Canadensis

Canada goose lands on a marsh early in spring

When most North Americans think of geese, they think of Canada geese. As the most common species of goose on the continent, it is found practically everywhere.

APPEARANCE

Length 25–45 inches. Wingspan 43–68 inches. A large, heavy goose, gray-brown overall, with lighter undersides, a long black neck, black head, tail and bill and a striking white cheek patch. Great size differences exist among the various races of the species. The smallest, an Arctic species, is the size of a large duck, while the largest race may have nearly twice the wingspan and weigh almost three times as much.

HABITAT

Its habitats are ecologically diverse from vast, treeless areas in the Arctic to wetlands surrounded by heavy forests to prairie sloughs and coastal areas. Lakes, ponds, bogs, fens, large streams, urban ponds, wet meadows, swamps, freshwater and saltwater marshes are all utilized by the Canada goose. Grain and cornfields are also favored as a convenient source of food.

The range of the Canada goose

BEHAVIOR

The most famous behavior of the Canada goose is their habit of migrating in graceful V-formations accompanied by melancholic honking. It is very gregarious, and is found in flocks. It forages by reaching into the water to gather food, and also picks food directly from the surface or from the ground. When a flock is feeding, at least one bird will act as a sentry to warn the others of danger. It is well adapted for walking and swimming, and runs a short distance to gather speed before taking off. Flight is powerful.

CALLS

Call is a resonant double honk that sounds quite pleasant in a chorus and at a distance. The smallest race has a higher-pitched cackling sound.

FOOD

Diet consists mostly of vegetable matter such as the seeds of grasses and sedges, shoots of aquatic plants, berries, grains and corn. Also eats crustaceans, mollusks and other invertebrates.

FAMILY LIFE

Female builds a down-lined ground nest made of grasses, sticks and other vegetation, often in a high spot near water or on a small islet in a marsh or pond. Rarely an abandoned tree nest of an osprey may be used. Four to ten eggs are incubated for 25 to 30 days by the female. First flight occurs between 40 to 73 days, depending on the race. The young are tended by both parents and stay with them through their first winter until they return to the breeding grounds in the spring. One brood per year.

MIGRATION
Its perennial V-flight pilgrimage to the North in early spring and back again in late fall has made the Canada goose the archetype of migrating birds in North America. Spring birds arrive as the ice breaks up, generally from February to April. Fall migration generally occurs from September to December. In the southern part of its range, it is a year-round resident.

CONSERVATION CONCERNS
Species status overall in North America is secure and stable. The Canada goose is abundant and widespread across the continent despite being heavily hunted as a game bird. The Atlantic Canadian population appears to be declining. Although the Aleutian Canada goose of Alaska, subspecies *Leucopareia*, is listed as a federally threatened species in the United States, its population has increased

The familiar Canada goose is the quintessential wetland bird of North America

from only 800 in the 1960s to approximately 60,000 birds now. Another subspecies *Occidentalis*, the dusky Canada goose, is considered in peril of extinction in British Columbia, Oregon and Alaska.

RELATED SPECIES
Only the Brant, a somewhat similar and smaller goose that breeds in the high Arctic, shares the genus *Branta* with the Canada goose as a breeding bird in North America.

Did You Know?
The familiar V-formation of Canada geese and other species such as cormorants has evolved to help them save energy while in flight. In geese, the "V" puts them in a configuration where the air currents produced by the wings of a leading bird reduces the amount of drag behind and off to the sides, making flight easier for the flanking birds that follow. This may reduce energy expended by up to 50 percent. Obviously, the leading bird doesn't benefit and that's why the position is rotated regularly so all birds can take advantage.

WOOD DUCK

Aix sponsa

A female wood duck and her ducklings

In full breeding plumage, the male wood duck is the most beautiful of all North American ducks.

APPEARANCE
Length 18.5 inches. Wingspan 30 inches. The male is unlike any other North American duck. Its most prominent feature is the long, swept-back crest, which looks like an oversized helmet, and a defined U-shaped spur of white on the side of the head. The rest of the bird is an assortment of bright iridescent greens, blues and purples. The similarly shaped female is much duller than the male with an overall variegated brown accented by white stripes and iridescent blue patches. The head is gray with a prominent white eye-ring. Both sexes have long tails and short bills.

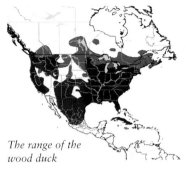

The range of the wood duck

HABITAT

A tree-loving duck, it prefers wooded wetlands such as swamps, ponds, lakes, streams and flooded forest.

BEHAVIOR

It is usually seen in pairs, less frequently in small flocks. It forages by gleaning food from the surface of the water. Very adept at walking on land, the wood duck often comes right out of the water to pick the seeds and acorns of shrubs, trees and other vegetation, and perches in trees. It takes off almost vertically from water with no running and flight is very rapid.

CALLS

Quite vocal. The male utters an upward pitching whistle, while the female gives a shrill *oo-weet, oo-weet* call when alarmed.

FOOD

Diet includes seeds, acorns, berries, beechnuts and wild rice. Also takes aquatic insects, mollusks and amphibians.

FAMILY LIFE

Nest is in a natural cavity or rotted-out branch of a tree. Occasionally nests in a cavity made by another species such as a pileated woodpecker. Will also nest in artificial nesting boxes. The female lines it with wood chips and down before laying ten to fifteen eggs, which she incubates for 28 to 37 days. Despite sometimes being placed 50 feet or higher, the newly hatched downy young will exit the nest by jumping to the ground unharmed. The mother tends the young for 56 to 70 days until their first flight. One or two broods per year.

MIGRATION

Migrant birds generally arrive on their breeding grounds in March or April. Fall migration occurs from mid-September to

November. In the southern part of its range the wood duck is a year-round resident.

CONSERVATION CONCERNS
Species status overall in North America is secure and its population is increasing. Hunted almost to extinction by the late nineteenth and early twentieth century. Fortunately, since the inception of the Canada–United States Migratory Bird Convention of 1916, the population has increased dramatically. Threats still face the species, especially the destruction of the wet forested habitats where it nests.

RELATED SPECIES
Although considered a "dabbling duck" along with ducks of the genus *Anas*, the wood duck belongs to its own separate genus *Aix*.

The male wood duck is the most spectacular North American wetland bird

A female wood duck shows just a hint of the male's brilliant colors

MALLARD

Anas platyrhynchos

The male mallard is one of the most recognizable ducks in North America

When many people hear the word "duck," they probably think of the mallard. This ubiquitous species continues to expand its range across the continent and is now found from coast to coast and from the Mexican border to the Arctic.

APPEARANCE

Length 23 inches. Wingspan 35 inches. A large, heavy duck, similar in size to the slightly heavier American black duck; the breeding male has a light gray body and belly, dark brown breast, a white neck-ring, bright yellow bill and iridescent green head. The female is a light mottled brown, with a dull orange bill and a dark stripe through the eye. Both sexes have a metallic blue patch on the trailing edge of the wing.

HABITAT

Although primarily a marsh duck, the mallard will inhabit almost any body of shallow water, including ponds, lakes, flooded forests and swamps. Although it is less inclined to breed in saltwater areas than its close relative, the black duck, it will often use salt marshes and sheltered bays during the winter.

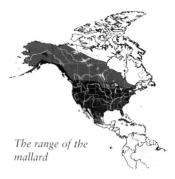

The range of the mallard

In winter it is common in city park ponds if it is artificially fed.

BEHAVIOR

Often seen in flocks. Less wary than the American back duck and an extremely adaptable species, the mallard will forage in almost any environment where the water depth is 12–16 inches. This is just deep enough to allow it to reach bottom with its bill using the "tip-up" technique so characteristic of dabbling ducks. Also frequents stubble fields where wasted grain or corn provides a convenient meal. Propelled by explosive wing beats, it takes off from the water almost vertically. Flight is rapid and direct.

CALLS

A loud, descending quack, quack, quack is given by the female, while the male's call is somewhat softer and higher-pitched.

FOOD

Will eat the seeds and shoots of aquatic vegetation such as sedges and grasses, waste grain and corn. Will also take animals such as mollusks, insects, crustaceans and will occasionally scavenge dead fish. Nesting females generally eat a greater percentage of animal food than males.

FAMILY LIFE

The female builds the nest of leaves, stems and grasses in a slight depression surrounded by dense vegetation such as cattails, reeds and rushes, and line with down. Occasionally nests in underbrush piles or in hollow trees. Nests are usually near water. Generally seven to ten eggs are incubated for 26 to 30 days. After the young hatch, the female tends them for 42 to 60 days until they can fly. The mallard is the ancestor of many varieties of domesticated ducks worldwide. Also hybridizes with American black ducks in the wild. One brood per year.

MIGRATION
Northern breeding birds generally arrive very early in spring during ice breakup from late February to early May. Fall migration is the most prolonged and can last from August to mid-December. Resident year-round throughout much of its range.

CONSERVATION CONCERNS
Species status overall in North America is generally secure and stable. Although harvested heavily by hunters, the mallard is still widespread and abundant despite declining numbers in the Prairies. Continues to expand its range eastward where it is hybridizing with the American black duck in many areas.

RELATED SPECIES
The two species most similar to the mallard are the American black duck and the mottled duck.

Female mallards are less flashy than their male counterparts

AMERICAN BLACK DUCK

Anas rupripes

American black duck takes off, showing the characteristic white area on the underside of the wing

This large, plain duck is generally the most common freshwater duck species in eastern North America.

APPEARANCE
Length 23 inches. Wingspan 35 inches. One of the heaviest and largest of the dabbling ducks, the male is a sooty blackish-brown with a yellow bill. The neck and head are a mottled gray. The female is slightly more brownish (but still quite dark) overall with a dull olive bill. The edges of the feathers are buff-colored in both males and females. Both sexes have a purple speculum patch that is sometimes visible when not in flight, but more apparent in flight. Undersides of the wings show bright white.

HABITAT

The black duck is a habitat generalist and is found in freshwater and saltwater marshes, wet meadows, fens and the shallow edges of lakes, ponds and sluggish streams. It is the most common duck

of salt marshes of the Atlantic Coast. In winter it lives in coastal bays and inlets, where it feeds on mudflats and in the shallows.

The range of the American black duck

BEHAVIOR

One of the wariest, most skittish ducks, it is extremely difficult to approach and is on a constant lookout for danger. In addition to foraging like other marsh ducks by tipping up and dipping its bill into the water to pick up vegetation, the black duck also takes mollusks (blue mussels are a favorite), crustaceans and insects either from mudflats or shallow water. Extremely powerful, taking off from water or dry land, practically exploding into the air in very rapid flight. Often seen in small groups in the summer and large flocks during winter.

American black ducks

CALLS

The female has a very loud *quack*. Occasionally a comical series of *quacks* that sounds like a duck laugh can be heard. The male has a lower and softer *quack* than the female.

FOOD

Aquatic vegetation, grasses, grains, seeds, mollusks, crustaceans, tadpoles, insects and rarely small fish.

FAMILY LIFE

The female builds the nest of leaves, stems and grasses on the ground; lined with down. It seldom nests in hollow trees or old crows' nests. Generally eight to eleven eggs are incubated for 23 to 33 days. After the young hatch the female tends them for 58 to 63 days until they can fly. The black duck often hybridizes with mallards. Usually one brood per year.

MIGRATION

Generally arrives on breeding grounds in March or April, soon after the winter thaw. Southward migration occurs between September and November. Year-round resident over a large part of its range.

American black duck stretching on a hummock

CONSERVATION CONCERNS

Species status overall in North America is secure but population is declining significantly. Population went from 7 million 1955 to only 3 million in 1985. Overhunting, habitat loss and increased competition from the mallard (which continues to expand its range into traditional black duck areas) are contributing to the decline.

RELATED SPECIES

The mallard and the mottled duck are the most similar in habit and size.

A conservation status map of the American black duck

NORTHERN PINTAIL

Anas acuta

A female northern pintail

Elegant and beautiful, as well as hardy, this distinctive bird is one of the most common duck species in North America.

APPEARANCE
Length 21 inches. Wingspan 34 inches. A large, slender duck; the male in breeding plumage has a brown head, white breast and neck stripe, long pointed tail and slate blue sides. Both sexes have bluish-gray legs and bill and a very long neck and legs. The female is mottled, buff brown overall, light underneath and lacks the pintail of the male.

HABITAT
Freshwater marshes are preferred, but also shallow ponds and lakes and brackish marshes along the coast. Often rests in rafts on

53

ocean bays during the winter and occasionally feeds on mudflats when food is in short supply in its usual feeding areas. In winter it can often be found in agricultural fields and other upland areas where grain or seeds are available.

The range of the northern pintail

BEHAVIOR

Forages in typical dabbling duck fashion by tipping forward into the water to gather food in its bill. Because of its long neck, it is able to feed in areas too deep for other dabbling ducks.

Will gather into dense flocks in favored southern marsh habitats during winter, sometimes numbering in the tens of thousands. An extremely rapid and powerful flier with a spectacular habit of practically dropping out of the sky and into the marsh in an apparently uncontrolled, twisting descent.

CALLS

The male has a thin, almost buzzy *zweeaa* call heard year round and a low double whistle normally given in breeding season. The female has a typically ducky *quack* similar to a mallard or black duck female.

A male northern pintail in breeding plumage

FOOD
Mostly the seeds of aquatic vegetation, but occasionally may eat snails and other tiny shellfish.

FAMILY LIFE
The female builds a nest on the ground, usually near water and sometimes concealed by surrounding vegetation. Occasionally a nest is built on open prairie near a slough. Six to twelve eggs are incubated by the female for 22 to 25 days. The young leave the nest hours after hatching and are able to fly after 36 to 57 days. One brood per year.

MIGRATION
An early northern migrant, often arriving in March just after the ice has melted on lakes and ponds. Most pintails have departed the vicinity of their northern breeding grounds by late fall.

CONSERVATION CONCERNS
Species status in North America is secure and stable.

RELATED SPECIES
The northern pintail is one of the twelve dabbling duck species that breed in North America.

Did You Know?

Most groups of species can be characterized by how they get food. Wetlands are homes to two such categories of ducks: the dabblers and the divers. Dabblers have longer legs placed farther forward on the body and gather food by skimming the surface with their bills or tipping their bodies forward to reach into the shallows for food—they are also known as "tip-up" ducks. Dabblers include all ducks of the genus *Anas* such as mallards, black ducks, northern pintails and teals. Divers have short powerful legs placed farther back on the body for swimming and typically will dive underwater to retrieve food. This group includes, among others, ring-necked ducks, lesser and greater scaups and canvasbacks.

NORTHERN SHOVELER

Anas clypeata

The male northern shoveler is one of the most colorful dabbling ducks

The comical-looking Northern Shoveler, with its outsized bill and bright colors, is one of the most beautiful ducks found in North America's wetlands.

APPEARANCE
Length 19 inches. Wingspan 30 inches. A medium-sized duck with a huge spatulate bill and a short neck. On the water, it tends to ride low in the front. In breeding, the male has a dark green iridescent head, white breast, a blue patch on its side and rufous-red belly and sides; the bill is black. The northern shoveler male shows more white than any other species of dabbling duck. The female is overall mottled brown with a dull orange bill. Both sexes have yellow eyes.

HABITAT
Inhabits shallow freshwater lakes, sloughs, marshes, ponds and mud flats, especially areas with abundant plant and animal life on the surface. It is also found in brackish marshes. Areas with heavy vegetation that provides cover are preferred.

The range of the northern shoveler

BEHAVIOR
Compared to other dabbling duck species the northern shoveler is quite bold and relatively easy to approach. Shovelers do not tip their bodies forward to feed but instead paddle around with their bills submerged in the water. Often feed in small groups. Tiny plants and animals are strained from the mud through little comb-like structures on either side of the bill called lamellae, however they do pick larger items directly from the water. Flight is very rapid and landings are often preceded by an abrupt descent.

CALLS
Less vocal than many duck species. The male's call is a low, guttural croak of *hwuh-hwuh*. The female has a weak, nasal *quack*.

FOOD
Aquatic vegetation such as duck-weed, milfoil and plankton. In addition, about one-third of the diet consists of insects, crustaceans, worms and mollusks.

FAMILY LIFE
The female builds a nest in a slight hollow where it is concealed by long grass, usually near water. Grasses and down are used to line the nest. Generally nine to twelve eggs are incubated by the female for 22 to 25 days and are tended by the female for 38 to 66 days until they can fly. One brood per year.

MIGRATION

Generally arrives on its breeding grounds in late March or early April and departs on its southerly migration in late September or early October.

CONSERVATION CONCERNS

Species status overall in North America is secure and stable. Population in the U.S. is apparently secure but there are some concerns about declines in Canada. More recently, the species has been expanding its range to the east.

A conservation status map of the northern shoveler

RELATED SPECIES

There are eleven other ducks in the genus *Anas* including, among others, the mallard, American black duck, and blue-winged and green-winged teals.

The enormous bill is the most distinguishing mark of the northern shoveler

BLUE-WINGED TEAL

Anas discors

A male blue-winged teal in breeding plumage

This small and lovely duck's unwary nature makes it relatively easy to approach compared to most waterfowl species.

APPEARANCE

Length 16 inches. Wingspan 24 inches. Slightly larger than the smallest dabbling duck, the green-winged teal male in breeding plumage has a gray head and upper neck with a purplish hue, a brilliant white crescent around the front of the face and a black bill. The lower body is a warm pinkish-brown with black speckling and the sides have a conspicuous white flank patch toward the rear. Female is brown with a grayish head and whitish chin. In addition to an iridescent green speculum, both sexes have a large pale blue patch on the leading edge of the wing.

HABITAT

Well-vegetated shallow marshes, lakes, ponds, sloughs, sluggish streams, mudflats and other wetlands are preferred. Seldom visits salt marshes and brackish environments.

The range of the blue-winged teal

BEHAVIOR

Usually seen in pairs or small flocks. Prefers shallow water where it forages by reaching out with its bill to pick bits of food from the surface, as well as occasionally tipping up to get food in deeper water; some reports of foraging by diving. Takes off directly and powerfully from the water and has a very rapid flight. Small flocks are often seen twisting and wheeling in flight in perfect, close unison. The female will feign injury to draw predators away from her young.

CALLS

The male's call is a thin *seep*, while the female has a high, weak *quack*.

FOOD

Most of its diet is made up of sedges, pondweeds, duckweed and grasses. Also eats snails, crustaceans and other invertebrates.

FAMILY LIFE

Female builds a ground nest of grasses and other soft plant matter lined by down. Nest is often concealed by surrounding vegetation, usually near water. Generally eight to eleven eggs are incubated by the female for 23 to 27 days. The young are tended by the female. Because they have one of the shortest breeding seasons of any dabbling duck, the young develop quickly, making their first flight after only 35 to 44 days. One brood per year.

MIGRATION

Spring migrants generally arrive on breeding grounds from March to May. Fall migration occurs from mid-August until mid-October. Almost the entire population (possibly over 90 percent) winters south of the United States.

CONSERVATION CONCERNS

Species status overall in North America is secure; population is possibly increasing; quite common. The population appears fine. However, given the proportion of blue-winged teals that winter in Central and South America (the highest of all dabbling ducks), it is difficult to determine how much habitat destruction and hunting there threatens the population.

RELATED SPECIES

Closest relative is the cinnamon teal with whom it hybridizes. The females of green-winged and blue-winged teals are quite similar.

Blue-winged teal female

GREEN-WINGED TEAL

Anas crecca

A male green-winged teal shows off its chestnut-brown head with brilliant green accents

One of the smallest North American ducks, the little green-winged teal is a robust species nonetheless, arriving earlier in northern areas in spring and leaving later than most species.

APPEARANCE

Length 14 inches. Wingspan 23 inches. This stocky little duck is about the size of a rock dove (common pigeon). The male is one of the most beautiful ducks with a deep chestnut-brown head, a black bill and a vivid green patch running from the eye to the back of the neck. A white vertical slash separates the breast from the sides, and the breast is spotted. The female is a mottled dark brown. Both sexes have gray legs and a bright green patch on the trailing edge of the wing that is visible in flight.

HABITAT

Inhabits freshwater marshes, lakes, ponds and sloughs. Areas with dense aquatic vegetation are preferred. Occasionally spends time on saltwater and brackish marshes during migration and in the winter.

The range of the green-winged teal

BEHAVIOR

Often seen in small loose flocks. As a tip-up duck, it forages by leaning its body forward and reaching into the water to pick food with its bill. Is quite wary and difficult to approach. Flocks are often in formation during flight. Flies at a very high speed and with great agility. A flock can change direction in unison, almost instantaneously.

CALLS

The male green-winged teal has a distinctive short whistle. Females have a feeble *quack*.

FOOD

Primarily seeds of aquatic vegetation, but also stems and leaves. Aquatic insects, crustaceans, mollusks and tadpoles are also taken.

FAMILY LIFE

Female builds the nest on the ground using twigs, grasses, leaves and feathers, lined with down. Nest is often close to water, but occasionally a fair distance from it. Generally eight to twelve eggs are laid and incubated by the female for 21 to 23 days. Young grow extremely quickly and make their first flight after about 34 days. One brood per year.

MIGRATION

The widely distributed green-winged teal generally arrives on breeding grounds in late April to mid-May (earlier in southern parts of its range). After breeding, quite a large number of them may be seen in September to November in coastal marshes where they congregate to feed prior to heading south.

CONSERVATION CONCERNS
Species status overall in North America is secure and stable.

RELATED SPECIES
Of the eleven other ducks belonging to the genus *Anas*, the blue-winged teal is the most similar in size and appearance to the green-winged teal.

A male green-winged teal rears up to stretch its wings

Female green-winged teal

RING-NECKED DUCK

Aythya collaris

A male (left) and female ring-necked duck pair

This big-headed, little bird is the most widely distributed and commonly seen freshwater diving duck across much of the continent.

APPEARANCE
Length 17 inches. Wingspan 25 inches. Floats quite high in the water. Male is black on top and on the breast. The silvery gray sides are separated from an upper dark area by a distinctive horizontal crescent. The blackish head has a dark purple iridescence (not always visible) and appears peaked at the back. Bill is bluish-gray with a narrow white ring at the base and a wider one near the tip. The female is overall brown, a little darker on the top with a similar but faint curve delineating the lighter sides from the top. The chestnut-colored ring around the neck of the male is impossible to see except at very close range.

HABITAT

Prefers tree-lined freshwater marshes with dense vegetation and the shallows of lakes and ponds and slow-moving streams. Is frequently found in wooded swamps. Takes advantage of areas with water too deep for dabbling ducks. Often breeds in low-productivity habitats (i.e., highly acidic) avoided by other duck species. Occasionally visits salt water.

The range of the ring-necked duck

BEHAVIOR

Usually found in pairs or small flocks. Forages by taking short dives to considerable depths. Less wary than many other duck species and will usually fly only a short distance when frightened. Unlike the dabbling ducks, ring-necked ducks must run a short distance across the water before getting airborne.

CALLS

The male is usually silent except during breeding season when it has a low-pitched purring call. The female has a grating growl.

FOOD

Diet consists primarily of seeds and leaves of aquatic vegetation such as sedges, pond lilies and grasses. Ringed-neck ducks also consume aquatic insects, mollusks and other invertebrates.

FAMILY LIFE

The female builds its nest on the ground at the water's edge using the surrounding marsh vegetation and lines it with down. Occasionally will build a floating nest. The construction of the nest does not generally begin in earnest until the third or fourth egg is laid. Generally eight to ten eggs are laid which are incubated by the female for 25 to 29 days. After hatching, the young are tended by the female. The young take their first flight after about 50 days. One brood per year.

A pair of ring-necked ducklings feeding on aquatic vegetation

MIGRATION

Spring migrants generally arrive on their breeding grounds in the latter half of March or April and begin their fall journey south in late October or November. There is a year-round population in a small range in the Pacific Northwest and southern British Columbia.

CONSERVATION CONCERNS

Species status overall in North America is secure and stable. The ring-necked duck is quite common in North America and its population may be increasing over much of its range, although its numbers appear to be declining in wintering areas.

RELATED SPECIES

In addition to the ring-necked duck, there are five species of regularly breeding freshwater diving ducks in the genus *Aythya* in North America, including the canvasback, redhead, lesser scaup and greater scaup.

Photographer's Journal

Ducks are the most wary of all wetland birds. Relentless sport hunting over the past century has made them understandably skittish. Their superb vision and constant vigilance means that even a careful approach in a well-camouflaged blind more often than not will fail. One of the real challenges photographing from a floating blind is that most of the time, approaching the subject has to be done right out in the open. There is nowhere to hide and you just have to hope that the birds eventually think you are part of the

A male ring-necked duck patters along the water before getting airborne

landscape—a muskrat lodge, a floating raft of cattails, etc. This fact is especially hard to brook when dealing with hair-trigger ducks. Here, I was intending to approach close enough to photograph an individual bird feeding. But, as often happens with ducks (and this makes them super-frustrating at times) it was spooked just as I was composing the shot. Luckily, however, I was looking through the viewfinder at the moment it took off. Although unplanned, it gave me, I think, a more unique picture. Sometimes you win when you lose!

Did You Know?

Some birds are virtually helpless when they hatch, while others are able to leave the nest and even feed themselves almost immediately. Altricial young are born naked, often with closed eyes and practically immobile. Species that are altricial include all passerines (songbirds) and herons. They require a lot of care and nurturing by parents before they are able to leave the nest. Precocial birds are born with eyes open, covered in down and are mobile enough to leave the nest very soon after hatching, usually within two days. Examples of precocial birds are shorebirds and ducks. In other species the young may be born with intermediate stages of development.

BUFFLEHEAD

Bucephala albeola

The striking male bufflehead is in stark contrast to the drab female

This remarkably tough bird, the smallest of all North American diving ducks, is equally at home on a raging winter ocean or a quiet inland lake.

APPEARANCE
Length 13 inches. Wingspan 21 inches. A very compact species with a relatively large head, hence the name Bufflehead (for Buffalo). Its small size may have evolved from its habit of nesting in the holes of northern flicker woodpeckers. The male is mostly white with a black back. The back of the purple and green-tinted head (appears black at a distance) is covered by a brilliant white patch. The female is dark grayish-brown overall, lighter on the top. A distinctive oval white patch is visible on the head, just behind and below the eye. Both sexes have a small bill and a relatively long tail.

HABITAT

Breeds in freshwater wetlands such as ponds and lakes that are near the mixed conifer-deciduous woodlands where it builds its nest. During winter, it is inclined to inhabit saltwater bays and other coastal areas.

The range of the bufflehead

BEHAVIOR

Usually seen singly or in small flocks. Forages by diving in shallow water of 5–13 feet deep to gather small animals from the bottom. This efficient underwater swimmer's dives will usually last only ten seconds or so. While feeding, all the birds in a group try to dive at the same time, as if each is afraid of being left alone on the surface. Unlike the other diving ducks, the bufflehead sometimes takes flight directly without running along the water, although occasionally short take-off runs of a few steps can be observed. Flight is extremely rapid with very fast, almost buzzing wing beats.

CALLS

The male has a squeaky, forced whistle and a rolling guttural note. Female utters a hoarse *quack*.

FOOD

The diet consists largely of animal food, including small fish (especially in saltwater habitats), aquatic insects, amphipods (tiny shrimp-like animals) and mollusks. Some seeds are also taken.

FAMILY LIFE

The female will line an old woodpecker nest cavity with down and feathers and will occasionally burrow into a natural embankment when tree cavities are scarce. Eight to ten eggs are incubated by the female for 28 to 33 days. The young leave the nest after about a day by jumping out of the hole, which is generally between 5–20 feet from the ground. The female will tend the young for 50 to 55 days until they make their first flight. One brood per year.

MIGRATION
In much of North America, including both coasts, the bufflehead is a wintering bird that will usually arrive in mid- to late fall and leave again by the end of the following April. Where it is a nesting species, it generally arrives in early April to early May. It departs its breeding grounds on fall migration in late October.

CONSERVATION CONCERNS
Species status overall in North America is secure with a stable population. The bufflehead may have been much more numerous before widespread hunting in the nineteenth and early twentieth centuries. While still quite common in North America overall, its numbers appear to be declining somewhat in the west. Continued clearcut logging in the boreal forest has reduced the number of nesting sites available, which reduces overall reproduction success in the species.

RELATED SPECIES
Although the bufflehead is the only species in its genus *Bucephala*, the larger common goldeneye and Barrow's goldeneye ducks are similar in appearance and habits.

One of the smallest of all ducks, buffleheads, such as this female, spend time on both wetlands and the ocean

HOODED MERGANSER

Lophodytes cucullatus

A female hooded merganser shows its crest

This small diving duck possesses a distinctive crest of feathers, which, when opened, gives the impression that the bird has an enormous head.

APPEARANCE
Length 18 inches. Wingspan 24 inches. The most distinguishing feature of this duck is a conspicuous crest that can be raised or lowered. When raised, the male's crest has a thick, teardrop-shaped area of white on the rear half of the head surrounded by black. When lowered, the teardrop becomes a thick white stripe beginning behind the eye and running to the back of the head. The back is black and the sides are a rich reddish brown. Two spurs of black run parallel down the side of the breast. The overall gray-and-brown female has a less flamboyant crest that lacks the distinctive

black-and-white contrast of the male. Both sexes have a short, thin "sawtooth" bill and a long tail.

HABITAT
Essentially freshwater habitats, including swampy forests, small woodland ponds, lakes and streams, but also estuaries. Like

The range of the hooded merganser

other merganser species, it can also be found on marshes occasionally and frequents saltwater bays, especially in winter.

BEHAVIOR
An expert diver that is as at home hunting in a still pond as it is in a swift stream. Swims underwater by using both its webbed feet and its wings to swiftly pursue prey. Uses its strongly serrated bill to seize small fish. Quickly rises from the surface of the water and flies rapidly. Normally seen in pairs in summer and in quite small flocks during winter. Is relatively tame and easy to approach.

CALLS
Male gives a low croaking *crooo* and chattering sounds. Female gives a low croak.

FOOD
Mostly small fish, crayfish, aquatic insects, crustaceans, mollusks and some plant matter.

FAMILY LIFE
The female lines a tree cavity usually near water, with grass, leaves and down. Usually ten to twelve eggs are laid, which she incubates for 32 or 33 days until hatching. Occasionally will use a nesting box intended for wood ducks. The young leave the nest within 24 hours of hatching. The female tends the young (which get their own food) until their first flight at 71 days. One brood annually.

WATERFOWL

MIGRATION
Normally arrives on its breeding grounds in March or April (earlier in southernmost breeding range). Many birds will stay quite late in the fall before migrating south, often not leaving until ponds freeze over.

CONSERVATION CONCERNS
Species status overall in North America is secure and stable. Population may be vulnerable to forestry practices that destroy nesting sites.

RELATED SPECIES
Closest relatives in North America are the red-breasted merganser and the common merganser.

The spectacular male hooded merganser. Note the "sawtooth" bill for capturing prey

WADING BIRDS

AMERICAN BITTERN

Botaurus letiginosis

An American bittern in heavy rushes

There is no sound in nature more unmistakable than the booming mating call of the male American bittern. Relatively little is known about its biology owing to its secretive nature.

APPEARANCE
Length 23 inches. Wingspan 45 inches. Its shape resembles a mottled and striped brown bowling pin, with a rather rotund body and a much shorter neck than most herons.

HABITAT
Fresh and saltwater marshes, wet meadows, damp alder and willow thickets. Thick vegetation such as cattails, bulrushes, reeds and long grass is preferred. Here its camouflage can be best put to use to evade predators.

BEHAVIOR

The range of the American bittern

One of the most characteristic behaviors of the American bittern is the way it attempts to hide from humans and predators alike. When alarmed it draws its feathers against its body to make itself appear smaller, points its bill straight up into the air and freezes in position, thus aligning its contour and stripes with the vertical vegetation that surrounds it, rendering it almost invisible.

Spending most of its time among the thick cattail swales or bulrushes, it stealthily stalks its prey, which it jabs it with a lightning-fast strike of its dagger-like bill.

CALLS

The male bittern's booming, mechanical *oong-ka' choonk*, or *oonck-a-tsoonck* song carries a very long distance and adds a pleasant mysteriousness to the atmosphere of the marsh.

FOOD

These generalists will take anything they can catch. Frogs, snakes, crayfish, small fish, grasshoppers, water bugs, mollusks, dragonflies and other small animals are among their prey.

FAMILY LIFE

The female American bittern builds a flimsy ground nest of sticks, cattails, reeds or grasses, generally surrounded by heavy vegetation. Usually four or five eggs are laid and the female incubates for 28 or 29 days. The young remain in the nest for about two weeks and are fed regurgitated food by the parents. One brood annually.

MIGRATION

Usually arrives on its breeding grounds in March and April, and fall migrations occur during September to November. It is a year-round resident on the Pacific Coast of the United States.

CONSERVATION CONCERNS

Species status overall in North America is apparently secure, but significantly declining throughout its range due to habitat loss. Very difficult to determine its population because of its highly secretive nature, which makes it a challenge to study.

RELATED SPECIES

It is the only member of the genus *Botaurus* in North America.

A conservation status map of the American bittern

An American bittern is striking a "hiding pose" by compressing its feathers and pointing its bill skywards

GREAT BLUE HERON

Ardea herodias

Great blue herons are patient hunters who stalk, then strike aquatic prey with a sharp bill

The great blue heron is North America's largest and most familiar long-legged wading bird. In many places it is incorrectly called a crane.

APPEARANCE
Length 4 feet. Wingspan 6 feet. Unmistakable—a very large gray or blue-gray bird with white-and-black accents, a long neck and stilt-like legs. The eyes and the long bill are yellow. The great blue has a distinctive profile in flight with an S-shaped neck and long, trailing legs. Sexes look alike.

HABITAT
Areas with water shallow enough to wade in along the edges of bays, salt marshes, freshwater marshes, lakes, river margins,

streams, mudflats, sloughs, ditches, ponds and lakes.

BEHAVIOR

Hunts by stealth. Thrusts its spear-like bill into the water with a quick uncoiling of the neck. Fish are normally caught crosswise in the bill, then swallowed head first.

The range of the great blue heron

Usually solitary feeders, but occasionally groups congregate where there is plenty of food. Will often aggressively chase other herons from a feeding area. According to some sources, the heron will occasionally pirate food from other species. The nineteenth-century artist John James Audubon tells a story of one such encounter with an osprey: "The heron soon overtook the hawk, and at the very first lunge made by it, the latter dropped its quarry, when the heron sailed slowly towards the ground, where it no doubt found the fish." Will often stalk and prey on rodents in upland fields during winter.

WADING BIRDS

CALLS

In addition to the guttural *crawwk*, other sounds in its limited repertoire include a long, drawn-out *kronk* and a short *onk*.

FOOD

Fish are favored, and quite large ones are often taken. Crabs, frogs, lizards, snakes, other birds (usually nestlings), mice, rats, grasshoppers, dragonflies and occasionally baby alligators are also eaten. Adult alligators are also known to eat herons!

FAMILY LIFE

Nests in colonies of up to hundreds of pairs, usually located in trees near a good source of food, often on islands or in swampy areas. Rarely nests on the ground. The pair builds a large nest of sticks and twigs, lined with moss, grasses and leaves. Generally three to five eggs are incubated for about 28 days. Young are fed regurgitated food by both parents. After 56 to 60 days the young leave the nest and are fed by the parents for another 14 to 21 days before becoming independent. One brood per year.

A great blue heron in flight showing its full under-carriage

MIGRATION
Spring migration begins in February, and the last to arrive are northern breeders in late April or May. Birds leave on fall migration by September and October. Most great blue herons overwinter in the southern United States and Mexico. Breeders in the southern U.S. and many West Coast areas are nonmigratory, year-round residents.

CONSERVATION CONCERNS
Species status overall in North America is secure and stable or increasing population. However, *Ardea herodias fannini,* a darker race of the species on the West Coast of Canada, as well as the great white heron of Florida, are both considered vulnerable due to habitat loss and a small population, respectively.

RELATED SPECIES
The only other species in North America in the genus *Ardea* is the great egret.

Photographer's Journal

It is always a thrill to photograph the great blue heron at close range. As one of the largest of all the wetland birds, it is an impressive subject seen up close. Happily, great blues are relatively easy to approach in a floating blind. After about thirty minutes carefully approaching this one, the heron got accustomed to my presence, and I was able to get very close. Like many times before, I actually had to back up as this great blue began moving in my direction. It was completely oblivious of me, and almost came too close to photograph with a telephoto lens. This photo was made as the bird was strutting straight at me.

Did You Know?

Larger species of birds generally live longer. Although it is difficult to determine exactly what the life span of any given species is in the wild, estimates of the average age based on banded individuals give us a rough idea. The great blue heron is one of the longest lived of all wild birds with a maximum age in the wild of over twenty-three years! The red-winged blackbird lives to almost sixteen years, while the smaller tree swallow has a maximum age in the wild of only eleven years.

The largest North American heron is the great blue

GREAT EGRET

Ardea alba

A great egret foraging at the edge of the shallows

This large elegant bird, with its filamentous plumes and graceful movements, make it one of the highlight species of the wetlands.

APPEARANCE
Length 39 inches. Wingspan 51 inches. A long-necked, long-legged wading bird, somewhat smaller than a great blue heron, the great egret's pure white plumage, yellow bill and completely black legs and feet make it unmistakable. In breeding plumage, long, lacey feathers grow from the back, often extending beyond the tail. Sexes look similar.

HABITAT
Freshwater marshes, salt marshes, swamps, saltwater lagoons and shores, margins of lakes and ponds, sluggish streams and mudflats.

BEHAVIOR

Stalks prey in shallow water along the edges of streams, ponds, freshwater and saltwater marshes. During the day it feeds alone or in small groups; is often associated with other long-legged waders such as great blue herons, snowy egrets and tri-colored herons. At night, roosts communally in trees, which are shared with other heron and egret species. In flight, it exhibits the trademark bent S-shape neck of most herons. In the breeding rookery egrets are very territorial and strike postures to warn off intruders.

The range of the great egret

CALLS

The only sound uttered is a hoarse, rattling croak.

FOOD

Eats almost anything in or very near the water, including aquatic insects, snakes, frogs, crayfish, crabs and fish. Occasionally becomes prey for alligators in the southern habitats.

A great egret is majestic in flight

FAMILY LIFE

Nests colonially in rookeries with other heron species. Some colonies may contain hundreds of breeding pairs. Built by both sexes, the nest is a crudely made platform of small sticks often placed quite high up (when possible) in a tree in a swamp or a willow thicket. Male and female participate in the incubation of the usual three eggs until they are hatched after about 25 days. The young make their first flight after 42 to 49 days days. One brood per year.

MIGRATION

In the southern part of its range along the California, Gulf of Mexico and Florida coasts, the egret is a year-round resident. Generally arrives at its northern breeding areas in late February to mid-May. By late October or November most birds have left to overwinter in the southern United States and southward.

CONSERVATION CONCERNS

Species status overall in North America is secure and stable in the U.S., but vulnerable because of its limited range in Canada. In the nineteenth and early twentieth century the egret was almost hunted to extinction for its feathers. The widespread use of DDT in its habitat also had a negative effect on the population, but its numbers rebounded after DDT was banned.

RELATED SPECIES

The most closely related species is the great blue heron, which belongs to the same genus *Ardea*.

Did You Know?

Millions of birds were killed in the 1880s and early 1900s to supply feathers to the hat trade. The great egret and the snowy egret suffered the greatest losses due to their elegant plumes. In 1900, the enormous millinery trade (as the hat trade was known) employed 83,000 people in the U.S. Only after years of vigorous campaigning by conservationists against the killing did the practice of slaughtering birds for fashion end by 1920.

SNOWY EGRET

Egretta thula

A snowy egret carries itself in flight like other herons

Its small, delicate frame and pure white "cross aigrette" plumes makes the snowy egret the most elegant of all the North American herons. This exquisite plumage also helped bring it close to extinction in the early part of the century as it was hunted mercilessly for its feathers for the millinery (hat) trade. Fortunately, due to long-standing laws protecting wading birds, today its population is healthy and widespread.

APPEARANCE

Length 24 inches. Wingspan 41 inches. This small, slender, pure white heron has long, filamentous plumes on the back of the head and neck, the rump area and the front of the neck just above the breast, with black legs. Bright yellow feet are a distinguishing field mark. Black bill, yellow eyes and lores. Flies with a bent S-shaped neck and trailing legs.

The range of the snowy egret

HABITAT
Freshwater marshes, salt marshes, ponds, lakes, wet meadows, drainage ditches and canals, shallow coastal wetlands, streams and occasionally on open beaches or dry upland fields.

BEHAVIOR
Is one of the most active of herons while feeding. In shallow water, it vibrates its feet on the bottom to flush prey, then pursues it vigorously by running and dodging, often with its wings partially raised. Can be quite tame when accustomed to humans, often hanging around the beach or pier waiting for handouts of unwanted small fish from fishermen. Occasionally follows ibises through the water to feed on prey they've stirred up.

CALLS
Largely silent except for an occasional grating *craawwk*.

FOOD
Small fish, crustaceans such as crayfish and shrimp, frogs, other aquatic invertebrates and insects.

FAMILY LIFE
Nests in colonies with its own and other heron species. Both male and female participate in building a flat nest of sticks lined with soft plant material in a low bush or shrub. Generally three to five eggs are incubated by both sexes for 20 to 24 days. The young are fed by both parents for 30 days until their first flight.

MIGRATION
Is a year-round resident throughout much of its southern coastal

range in North America. Inland and more northerly breeders often migrate to the coast during winter. Snowy egrets often wander quite far north in the nonbreeding season.

CONSERVATION CONCERNS
Species status overall in North America is secure and stable. The snowy egret's population and range have expanded dramatically since they were protected from hunting in the early twentieth century. Continues to expand its range northward.

RELATED SPECIES
Its closest relatives are the little blue heron, the reddish egret and the tri-colored heron, all of which belong to the same genus *Egretta*.

Did You Know?
Some birds follow others around the wetland as a feeding strategy. This commensal relationship (when one species unwittingly helps another find food, but to no detriment to itself) is made up of "beaters" and "attendants." Beaters stir up prey animals and the attendants tag along, snapping up the excess. A well known beater/attendant pair in North American wetlands are white ibises and their attendant snowy egrets.

A snowy egret showing off its yellow feet

REDDISH EGRET

Egretta rufescens

Reddish egrets are the rarest of the heron species in North America

Stunning in its breeding plumage, the relatively rare reddish egret is a thrilling sight as it rushes to and fro, practically crashing through the shallows in pursuit of prey.

APPEARANCE
Length 30 inches. Wingspan 46 inches. This medium-sized, largely bluish gray heron has a head and neck of reddish brown. The back of the head appears shaggy with short, cascading plumes. It has a pink bill with a black tip and the legs are dark gray. In flight the neck is bent in an S-shape and legs trail behind. Sexes look similar. There is also a much less common pure white morph of the reddish egret.

HABITAT
Prefers shallow saltwater areas of the coast such as brackish and

salt marshes, lagoons and man-groves.

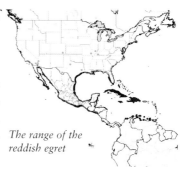

BEHAVIOR
Is less stealthy than other herons in its technique for acquiring food and very gracefully runs about in shallow water, frequently using its wings for balance while hunting schools of small fish in the shallows. Is extremely light on the wing and graceful in flight.

The range of the reddish egret

CALLS
A guttural *crawwk* that sounds a little less harsh than the calls of other herons.

FOOD
Fish, crustaceans and other aquatic invertebrates, most, if not all, of it obtained in salt water.

FAMILY LIFE
Nests in colonies, often with other species such as herons, spoonbills and cormorants. Both sexes build a flat platform nest of sticks and twigs in the tops of low bushes and shrubs (occasionally on the ground), often on coastal islands. Generally three or four eggs are laid which are incubated by both sexes for 25 or 26 days. The young are fed and tended by both parents for 45 days before they make their first flight. One brood annually.

MIGRATION
Generally nonmigratory.

CONSERVATION CONCERNS
Species status overall in North America is apparently stable and secure, but is considered a species of special concern because there are only about 2,000 pairs of reddish egrets nesting in North

A conservation status map of the reddish egret

America, all of them in the United States. It was decimated during the plume-hunting era of the late nineteenth and early twentieth centuries and its numbers have never really rebounded. For a number of years this egret was extirpated from Florida as a breeding species, only to later re-colonize it on a small scale.

RELATED SPECIES

Its closest relatives are the little blue heron, the snowy egret and the tri-colored heron, all of which belong to the genus *Egretta*.

Reddish egrets are very active feeders and run around in shallow water in pursuit of prey

LITTLE BLUE HERON

Egretta caerulea

A little blue heron foraging in a swamp

This elegant cousin to the great blue heron is unmistakable in its monochrome dark slate-blue plumage and small size. It is one of the most common herons in its range.

APPEARANCE
Length 24 inches. Wingspan 40 inches. Traditional heron shape (including in flight with its neck drawn in an S-shape and feet trailing). Overall dark slate-blue (neck and head appear slightly maroon) with greenish-yellow legs and a bluish bill with a black tip. Sexes look alike. Appears stockier than the similarly sized tricolored heron with which it associates. First year little blues are pure white and often mistaken for snowy egrets.

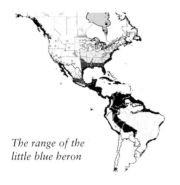

The range of the little blue heron

HABITAT

Found in a wide range of habitats, including freshwater marshes, ponds, lakes, inland streams, estuaries, mangroves and coastal marshes.

BEHAVIOR

Is retiring and shy, and stalks prey actively with measured footsteps in shallow water during daylight and darts out its spearlike bill to nab its meal. If food is plentiful, it occasionally runs through the water in pursuit. It is somewhat less active than snowy egrets or tri-colored herons—this may be a result of a higher proportion of slow-moving crustaceans and shellfish and fewer fish in its diet. Is light on the wing and graceful in flight. Often travels in small flocks and roosts in trees at night.

CALLS

Usually silent but occasionally gives low clucking notes. Is quite vocal during nesting and when alarmed gives a hoarse *crawwwk* sound.

FOOD

Crabs, crayfish, lizards, frogs, fish, aquatic invertebrates and insects.

FAMILY LIFE

Nests in colonies of various sizes, often with other heron species. Both parents participate in building a flimsy, slightly cupped nest of twigs and sticks, usually above water in dense thickets, but also in larger trees found in swampy areas. The usual two to five eggs are incubated by both adults for 20 to 23 days. The young are fed regurgitated food by both adults for 42 to 49 days before fledging. One brood annually.

MIGRATION

Is generally a year-round resident or migrates only a short distance within the southern United States. Like many heron species with southerly ranges, the little blue (particularly the white-plumaged juvenile) is often reported far to the north of its normal range (into Canada) outside of the breeding season.

CONSERVATION CONCERNS
Species status in North America is secure and stable. Its less "desirable" feathers meant it was less affected by plumage hunting in the late nineteenth and early twentieth centuries. May be vulnerable to the loss of nesting habitat.

RELATED SPECIES
Its closest relatives are the snowy egret, the reddish egret and the tri-colored heron, all of which belong to the same genus *Egretta*.

The little blue heron showing its deep blue plumage

TRI-COLORED HERON

Egretta tricolor

A tri-colored heron stalks its prey in deeper water

This slender and agile bird is one of most abundant and beautiful herons. The ornithologist Arthur Bent wrote, "For harmony in colors and grace in motion this little heron has few rivals."

APPEARANCE

Length 26 inches. Wingspan 36 inches. A medium-sized heron, this is the only heron that is dark above and white below. Its head, neck and bill are very slender and the red-orange eyes are distinctive. Upperparts are slate blue, underparts white, with yellow legs. Flies in typical heron fashion with the neck bent in an S-curve with legs and feet trailing behind.

HABITAT

Salt marshes, freshwater marshes and meadows (especially near the coast), ponds, lakes, rivers, estuaries and mangroves. Is particularly fond of open areas.

BEHAVIOR

Is a very active feeder in shallow water, moving, crouching and freezing frequently to survey the water for prey before striking with a lightning-quick thrust of its bill. Will often run through the water in pursuit of darting fish. Often feeds in somewhat deeper water, immersing up to it belly. Sometimes stirs the bottom with its feet to flush prey from the mud and often feeds on terrestrial insects in vegetation along waterways. Is quite deliberate in its movements; wary and flees easily at the sight of humans.

The range of the tri-colored heron

CALLS

Tri-colored herons give a variety of hoarse and gutteral croaks, the most common being a fairly quiet *awwk*.

FOOD

Fish, aquatic and terrestrial insects, worms, tadpoles, frogs, crayfish, lizards and leeches.

FAMILY LIFE

Nests in colonies with other tri-coloreds exclusively or with other heron species. Both adults participate in building a flat nest of sticks and twigs lined with soft plant material, usually in a low bush or tree near or over the water.

Generally three or four eggs are laid, which are incubated for 21 to 25 days by both adults. Both parents tend and feed the young regurgitated food for 35 days until they can fly. One brood annually.

MIGRATION

Is exclusively a southern bird, sometimes wintering as far south as Panama, and is largely a year-round resident within its range.

WADING BIRDS

However, it will wander within its range in search for food. Rarely moves north of its range along the coasts of the southern United States.

CONSERVATION CONCERNS
Species status overall in North America is secure and stable. May be declining due to the extensive loss of coastal salt marshes.

RELATED SPECIES
The tri-colored heron's closest relatives are the reddish egret, the snowy egret and the little blue heron, all of which share the genus *Egretta*.

The tri-colored heron is a striking and elegant bird

GREEN HERON

Butorides virescens

A green heron stalks through dense vegetation in the swamp

This widespread little heron is the most colorful bird in its family. Though shy by nature, it is rather tame and quite easily observed in the proper habitat.

APPEARANCE
Length 18 inches. Wingspan 26 inches. This small, stocky, dark heron has a dark blue-green back. The lower half of the head, the neck and the upper breast are a dark reddish brown. The head is capped by a dark blue-green cap. The neck is short and bittern-like. Legs are orange and relatively short and the wings are short and rounded.

HABITAT
Marshes, both freshwater and salt, the edges of ponds, slow-moving streams, swamps and mangroves. Prefers habitat that is edged by

The range of the green heron

trees or shrubs such as alders and mangroves.

BEHAVIOR
Can be relatively tame and easy to approach. Forages by standing still or stalking slowly through the water in typical heron style and stabbing its prey. Will also often fish from a low perch such as a snag. Has been known to put bits of bait or food on the water to attract prey. When alarmed, it will stretch out its neck and raise the feathers on its head, creating a disheveled crest.

CALLS
The main call is a harsh, abrupt *kyow*. A number of other squawks and grunts are also uttered.

FOOD
Diet is made up primarily of fish, but also includes invertebrates such as crabs, crayfish, aquatic and terrestrial insects.

FAMILY LIFE
Are usually solitary nesters, but are occasionally found in small colonies. Both adults build a flimsy nest of small sticks and twigs from 10–20 feet up in a small tree or less frequently on the ground or on a tussock in cattails, reeds or rushes. The two to four eggs are incubated by both sexes for 19 to 25 days. Young remain in the nest for 19 to 25 days and make their first flight after 34 or 35 days.

MIGRATION
Is migratory over most of its range within North America where it generally arrives on its breeding grounds in late March to mid-April and departs on its southerly migration in September or October. Is a year-round resident along the West Coast of the United States and in Florida.

CONSERVATION CONCERNS
Species status overall in North America is secure and stable with a possible decline in Canada.

RELATED SPECIES
The only species in genus *Butorides*. There are twelve species overall in *Ardidae*, the heron family.

A relatively small bird, the green heron is one of the two smallest heron species

YELLOW-CROWNED NIGHT HERON

Nyctanassa violacea

Somewhat nocturnal, yellow-crowned night herons will often perch for hours on end during the day in trees surrounding a wetland

The chunky little yellow-crowned night heron is occasionally active during the day when it can be seen skulking about the vegetation and the tangles of twigs that rim wooded wetlands.

APPEARANCE

Length 24 inches. Wingspan 42 inches. This medium-sized, short-necked heron has a body that is overall slate gray. The head is large and boldly patterned in black and white with a few long white plumes protruding from the back. The thick bill is black. Eyes are orange and the legs are dull yellow and quite long. Juveniles are mottled brown. In flight a slight S-bend in the neck is visible and the feet protrude past the tail. Sexes look similar.

HABITAT

Both saltwater and freshwater habitats; wooded swamps, freshwater and salt marshes, lagoons, tidal mud flats, mangroves, streams, lakes, ponds and occasionally in dry upland areas.

The range of the yellow-crowned night heron

BEHAVIOR

Is primarily a nocturnal hunter. Stalks prey in shallow water, on mudflats, or among branches or mangrove roots. Although generally nocturnal, it can often be seen during the day resting in a tree, but occasionally foraging as well. Is usually solitary. Juveniles are tamer than adults and more often seen during the day. Flight is not particularly strong.

CALLS

Commonly an abrupt *wawk* that is less harsh than other heron species.

WADING BIRDS

A juvenile yellow-crowned night heron under a mangrove tree at the edge of a salt marsh

FOOD
The yellow-crowned night heron is a crustacean specialist. Crabs and crayfish are most often taken, but it also eats fish, frogs, insects, leeches and occasionally will take small mammals and young birds.

FAMILY LIFE
Occasionally breeds in small, loose colonies and in larger mixed colonies, but is primarily a solitary nester. Both sexes build a substantial nest of sticks and twigs, usually placed in trees near water. Generally four or five eggs are incubated by both adults for 21 to 25 days. Young are fed by both parents for 25 days before leaving the nest. One brood annually.

MIGRATION
A short distance migrant, the yellow-crowned night heron generally arrives on its breeding grounds between mid-February to mid-April. Many birds wander north briefly in summer after the breeding season before migrating to southern areas later in the fall.

CONSERVATION CONCERNS
Species status overall in North America is secure and stable.

RELATED SPECIES
The other nocturnal heron in North America is the black-crowned night heron.

GLOSSY IBIS

Plegladis falcinellus

A glossy ibis showing why it is so named: The brightly colored iridescence (or glossiness) is apparent here

Although widespread across much of the eastern hemisphere, the glossy ibis may only be a relatively recent arrival to North America.

APPEARANCE
Length 23 inches. Wingspan 36 inches. Appears largely black at a distance. On closer inspection, particularly in the right light, the beautiful dark chestnut-brown body and the purple and dark blue-green iridescent wings can be seen. Has long downward curving brown bill, long greenish-brown legs and dark eyes. Flies with out-stretched neck and legs.

HABITAT
Freshwater and occasionally saltwater marshes, mudflats, swamps and wet meadows.

BEHAVIOR

The range of the glossy ibis

Is very gregarious, often seen foraging with the white ibis and other waders. Feeds in a methodical manner by using its long bill to probe the mud bottom in freshwater environments. When feeding, the glossy ibis is sometimes followed through the water by snowy egrets, who eat stirred up prey. Strong fliers, flocks travel by flapping and gliding in undulating strings through the sky, often in single file, or abreast. Is warier than the white ibis.

CALLS
Guttural croaking and a grunting *kruk kruk.*

FOOD
Crayfish, crabs, other aquatic invertebrates, small water snakes, leeches and insects.

Glossy ibis in flight showing full neck and leg extension

FAMILY LIFE
Nests in colonies with the white ibis and other wading birds. Both sexes build a large, cupped platform nest of sticks and twigs placed in low shrubs or trees over water, or on the ground. Generally two to four eggs are incubated mostly by the female for 21 days. Both parents feed the young in the nest for 28 days until their first flight. One brood annually.

MIGRATION
Largely resident within its range in North America, individuals occasionally wander as far north as eastern Canada and the northeastern United States.

CONSERVATION CONCERNS
Species status overall in North America is apparently secure and stable in the United States. Range is extending northward.

RELATED SPECIES
Closest relative in North America is the white-faced ibis belonging to the same genus *Plegladis*. The third species of ibis is the white ibis.

WHITE IBIS

Eudocimus albas

A white ibis feeds in a marsh

This distinctive white bird with its orange and red accents is one of the most abundant waders in southern wetlands.

APPEARANCE
Length 25 inches. Wingspan 38 inches. A large, pure white bird with long, orange-red legs, a long, very slender, downward-curving reddish bill, and an orange-red face (bright red during breeding season). Flies with its long neck and legs extended; black wing tips visible in flight.

HABITAT
Freshwater marshes, ponds, lakes, rivers and swamps. Generally prefers freshwater habitats, but can also be found in saltwater marshes and estuaries.

BEHAVIOR

Is a very active feeder that forages by probing its long de-curved bill into the mud in shallow water while walking and methodically sweeping it from side to side, enabling the bird to cover a large area. Often feeds among mangrove trees and in flooded swampy forests. Roosts in trees at night (some roosts are enormous with thousands of birds). They perform regular morning and evening flights to and from the feeding grounds in flocks (they can often be seen in a V-formation or strung out in single file in a long line). Flight is strong and swift with rapidly beating wings and occasional gliding. Often soars in circles.

The range of the white ibis

CALLS

A low nasal *hunk-hunk-hunk*.

FOOD

Crabs, crayfish, snails, insects, small water snakes and other aquatic and terrestrial invertebrates.

FAMILY LIFE

Nests in dense colonies with herons and other wading birds. Both adults participate in building a deeply cupped nest of sticks and twigs that is usually placed low in aquatic vegetation, trees or shrubs over the water. Generally two to three eggs are incubated by both sexes for 21 to 23 days. The young are fed by both parents for up to 35 days when they make their first flight.

MIGRATION

Is generally nonmigratory. Outside the breeding season, some individuals wander northward for a time.

WADING BIRDS

CONSERVATION CONCERNS
Species status in North America is secure and stable. Population has declined in Florida, but its range is expanding elsewhere.

RELATED SPECIES
The two other species of ibis breeding in North America, the glossy ibis and the white-faced ibis belong to a separate genus *Plegadis*.

A white ibis has brilliant white plumage

ROSEATE SPOONBILL

Platalea ajaja

A pair of roseate spoonbills in their habitat

The roseate spoonbill, with its long "spatulate"-shaped bill and its brilliant reddish-pink plumage, is one of the most remarkably beautiful birds in North America.

APPEARANCE
Length 32 inches. Wingspan 50 inches. This is a large reddish-pink wading bird. The only other pink bird that occurs in North America is the greater flamingo, which is rarely seen and doesn't breed here. The intensity of the color is variable depending on the bird's age (older birds are brighter) and diet. White neck, black band around back of head, featherless crown and forehead, and pink legs. Most unusual feature is the large bill that flares into a wide "spoon" at the end. Flies with its neck extended and legs trailing behind. Rarely glides in flight.

The range of the roseate spoonbill

HABITAT

Strong preference for salt or brackish water. Shallow salt-water lagoons, fresh water and salt marshes, mangroves and swamps, inland and along the coast.

BEHAVIOR

Is quite gregarious and forages in small groups by wading through the shallows. Sweeps its bill from side to side in long arcs through the water and mud while snapping up its prey. Sensitive bill detects food by feel. Is a strong flier with relatively slow, powerful wing beats. When traveling some distance, flocks often form a "V" in flight. Normally doesn't glide, but will occasionally soar on thermals like the wood stork.

CALLS

Is generally silent except for various grunts and croaks at their nesting rookeries.

The roseate spoonbill is spectacular in flight

FOOD

Small fish, shrimp, crayfish and other crustaceans, insects, other aquatic invertebrates and some plant material.

FAMILY LIFE

Breeds in small colonies with egrets and herons. Both sexes participate in building a deeply cupped nest of twigs and sticks among the branches of dense vegetation over water (occasionally on the ground). Generally three eggs are incubated by both adults for 22 or 23 days. Both parents feed the young for 35 to 42 days until they are able to fly. One brood annually.

MIGRATION

Is resident year round in its range and nonmigratory. Wanders short distances within its range to seek out favorable feeding conditions. Individuals often wander far to the north and west (as far north as Wisconsin and as far west as California) after the breeding season.

CONSERVATION CONCERNS

Species status overall in North America is apparently secure and stable in the United States.

RELATED SPECIES

Is the only spoonbill species found within North America.

The roseate spoonbill is showing off its namesake bill

WOOD STORK

Mycteria americana

A wood stork strolls along the edge of a saltwater lagoon

Its large, bare and wrinkled head, sedate movement and impressive stature gives one the impression that the wood stork is a "wise old bird."

APPEARANCE
Length 40 inches. Wingspan 61 inches. This very large, white bird has a long, heavy, de-curved bill and long, dark legs with pinkish feet, completely bare head and neck and a short black tail. There is considerable black on the trailing edge of the wings. Flies with neck and legs extended.

HABITAT
Lives both inland and along the coast in marshes, swamps, wet meadows, ponds, saltwater lagoons, marshes, mangroves and mudflats.

BEHAVIOR

A very active forager, individuals or groups of storks will often jump around in the water to stir up prey before walking through the shallows, sweeping their enormous bills through the water and gathering up practically every reasonably sized food item in their path. Using

The range of the wood stork

this method, the disturbed fish and crustaceans get snapped up on the surface or in mid-water. Normal flight is a combination of flapping and gliding. They perform spectacular aerial displays where groups spiral deep into the sky on warm thermals. Perches in trees.

CALLS

Silent except for hoarse croak given when disturbed. Very noisy in its nesting colony.

FOOD

Virtually any species that lives in or around shallow water: fish, frogs, crabs, crayfish, young alligators, snakes, insects and small turtles.

FAMILY LIFE

Nests in colonies of up to hundreds of birds. Both sexes participate in building a flimsy flat platform of large sticks, preferably placed high in the tops of bald cypress trees. Nest is lined with soft plant material. Generally three eggs are incubated by both adults for 28 to 32 days. Young are fed regurgitated fish by both parents for 55 to 60 days until they take their first flight. One brood annually.

MIGRATION

Resident throughout its range. Some individuals wander far to the north after breeding season, and wood storks are often seen in the northern United States and southern Canada.

CONSERVATION CONCERNS

Listed as an endangered species in the United States, the population is approximately 15,000 today, down from 150,000 in the early twentieth century. Loss of old growth bald cypress and other trees that are preferred as nesting sites is thought responsible for the decline. Loss of wood stork habitat due to the draining of large areas of the Everglades and other areas in Florida continues to be an issue.

A conservation status map of the wood stork

RELATED SPECIES

Is the sole stork species in North America.

Wood storks, despite their ungainly appearance, are very graceful fliers, even when coming in for a landing

LIMPKIN

Aramus guarauna

A limpkin in its usual habitat among the vegetation that grows along southern wetlands

Named for its unsteady limping gait, this largely nocturnal bird is more often heard than seen, and was formerly called the "crying bird" for its loud, rather unpleasant voice.

APPEARANCE
Length 26 inches. Wingspan 40 inches. The limpkin is a large brown, somewhat ibis-shaped bird, with white streaking and spots on its head, neck, back and wings, a fairly long, slightly downward-curving bill that actually curves to the right at the tip (perhaps an adaptation for eating its favorite food—snails) and long black legs. Flies with outstretched neck, dangling legs and weak wing beats.

HABITAT

Freshwater marshes, marshy stream and riverbanks, swampy woodlands and mangroves.

BEHAVIOR

Is normally solitary. Usually forages at night, but also during the day, by walking slowly through vegetation along the margins of

The range of the limpkin

marshes and streams probing its bill into the water to capture prey. Carries its body in a hunched-over position and twitches its tail when it walks. Spends much of the day resting in trees where it is quite adept at moving through the branches. Its flight is quite heavy and weak and it generally flees only a short distance when alarmed.

A limpkin is a seldom-seen species

It can become quite tame where it lives in close proximity to humans. However, birds in wilder areas remain very wary.

CALLS

Gives a rattling, guttural *kr-oww kr-oww* wail or scream, especially at night, considered one of the most haunting wild calls of any North American bird.

FOOD

Primarily large apple snails, but also other snails, mussels and other aquatic invertebrates, lizards, frogs, worms and insects.

FAMILY LIFE
Both sexes participate in building a loosely woven nest of the leaves and stems of emergent plants such as reeds and grass, usually concealed on the banks of streams, marshes or in clumps of vegetation over shallow water. Lined with fine plant material. Occasionally nests in trees. Generally four to eight eggs are incubated by both adults. Young are fed by one or both parents. Two to three broods annually.

MIGRATION
Resident year round throughout its range.

CONSERVATION CONCERNS
Species status overall in North America is vulnerable to extinction or extirpation in United States. Was extremely rare early in the twentieth century after being almost hunted to extinction. Numbers have increased, but are still relatively low.

RELATED SPECIES
No closely related species in North America.

A conservation status map of the limpkin

SANDHILL CRANE

Grus canadensis

A sandhill crane carries its body horizontally when foraging

The sandhill crane is one of the most statuesque, graceful and longest-lived of all wetland birds.

APPEARANCE
Length 45 inches. Wingspan 77 inches. This long-legged, long-necked, bird with a heavy body has plumage of a uniform gray. The head is adorned by a brilliant red crown and white cheeks. Legs are black. Bill is dark. The bird appears blunt at the rear end because of a "bustle" of tail feathers. Unlike herons, it flies with its neck outstretched. Sexes look similar.

HABITAT
Open marshes, bogs, prairies and wet meadows. In Florida it is found in open pine woodland with ponds and grassy areas, and is

occasionally seen on golf courses.

BEHAVIOR

The most notable behavior of the sandhill crane is its courtship dance. In small groups or in pairs, the birds will first raise their heads and walk around each other before bowing deeply and leaping 3 feet or

The range of the sandhill crane

more into the air with wings held loosely over their backs and feet thrust forward, only to land and do it again. They also run with their wings extended. Dance is accompanied by loud, rattling calls. Forages by strolling along and picking food items from the ground. Are very efficient walkers, often covering long distances while feeding. Flight is distinguished by very quick upstrokes, which contrast greatly with the lumbering strokes of a great blue heron.

CALLS

Is one of the most distinctive of all bird calls. Has a very powerful, deep, tremulous croak or trumpeting that sounds like *gur-ooo-ooo-ooo*. This remarkable sound carries a great distance and can often be heard before the bird can be seen.

FOOD

Is opportunistic, eating a wide variety of food—aquatic invertebrates, fish, snakes, frogs, other species of young birds and eggs, small mammals, insects, worms, and a variety of seeds, roots, berries, lichen, etc.

A sandhill crane adult and its chick

FAMILY LIFE

The nest, built by both adults, is a low mound of aquatic plants, often lined with grass or willow that is placed in shallow water or very damp conditions in marshy or boggy areas. Two eggs are laid, which are incubated by both parents for about 30 days before hatching. The young cranes, tended by both adults, will make their first flight after about 65 days. One brood per year.

A pair of sandhill cranes crossing bills

A conservation status map of the sandhill crane

MIGRATION

Migrates in large flocks and usually arrives at its breeding grounds in April or May. Fall migration occurs during September to November. In Florida there is a distinct breeding population that is resident year round.

CONSERVATION CONCERNS

Species status overall in North America is secure and increasing. However, the Mississippi sandhill crane, a subspecies, is critically endangered with between only 110 to 120 wild birds left and is listed as a federally endangered species in the United States. A captive breeding program has been used to bolster the population. Many of the Mississippi birds now in existence were born in captivity.

RELATED SPECIES

The highly endangered whooping crane, sharing the same genus *Grus*, is the only other crane species in North America. Worldwide there are fifteen species of cranes.

BIRDS OF PREY

OSPREY

Pandion haliaetus

Ospreys are one of the most spectacular species of wetland birds

The spectacular osprey, formerly the fish hawk, is the only North American raptor that eats fish exclusively.

APPEARANCE
Length 23 inches. Wingspan 63 inches. The osprey, a large hawk that looks somewhat like a gull from a distance, is mostly white below with some brown streaks, banding and stripes. Wings appear bent in flight. A dark area on the leading edge of the wing where it bends is visible. Is mostly dark brown above. Yellow eyes lack the characteristic heavy brow of other birds of prey. A thick black-brown stripe runs through the eye to the back of the head. Legs and feet are bluish gray. Sexes look similar.

The range of the osprey

HABITAT

Is found practically worldwide in both the northern and southern hemispheres. Lakes, ponds, slow-moving streams and rivers, and estuaries are their preferred habitats.

BEHAVIOR

Hovers 100 feet or so over the water and scans below for fish. Dives for fish by slamming into the water feet first, often submerging completely up to 3 feet deep. Seconds later it re-emerges with its prey and, with a few strokes of the wings, lifts into the air and flies back to its nest or a favorite feeding tree. It is timid and may flee at the slightest approach. This may be a legacy from the days when they were shot for "sport" in the 1800s and early 1900s before they were legally protected.

CALLS

Though generally a quiet bird, an osprey around the nest has a plaintive, repetitive *cheep-cheep-cheep* call. An even higher state of alarm is accompanied by a grating *creeee-kakakak*.

FOOD

Any species of fish is taken, provided they are near the surface and aren't too large. Catfish, suckers, herring, carp, shad, salmon, trout and others are on the menu. Ospreys go through an enormous amount of fish during the nesting season, requiring about 7 pounds every day to feed a brood of three young.

FAMILY LIFE

They are generally solitary nesters. Will occasionally nest in small, loose colonies where they are common. The nest, built by both parents, is a huge platform of large sticks up to 6 feet across and lined with twigs, grasses, moss and bark, usually placed in the tops of large, dead trees with a good vantage of the nearby water. Occasionally found on artificial nesting platforms and cliffs.

Generally two or three eggs are incubated mostly by the female for about 40 days. While sitting on the eggs the female relies on the male to bring her food. The young's first flight is in 7 or 8 weeks and 6 to 8 weeks after that they will catch their first fish. One brood per year.

MIGRATION
Arrives on summer breeding grounds in early March to May. By the end of September, most have migrated south to wintering grounds in Chile, Brazil and northern Argentina. Is year-round resident in Florida.

CONSERVATION CONCERNS
Species status overall in North America is secure and growing. The osprey is a good news story in bird conservation. Thanks to the banning of the pesticide DDT and the widespread provision of nesting platforms, the population has rebounded strongly from dangerously low levels in the 1950s to 1970s. The use of toxic chemicals in its wintering habitats in Central/South America is of continuing concern.

An osprey approaching its nest for a landing

RELATED SPECIES
There is only one species of osprey worldwide.

Photographer's Journal

Winging its way 100 feet or so over the water, an osprey will stop and hover on quick beating wings while scanning below for fish. Once a suitable fish is spotted near the surface, the osprey goes into action. With wings half folded, it plummets in a blur, slamming into the water head and feet first (the huge talons pushed forward up under the head) with a resounding splash, often submerging completely. In an instant, the osprey sinks its powerful talons into the unlucky fish, seizing it from behind. It re-emerges and, with a few mighty strokes of the wings, the bird lifts its soaked body and the writhing fish into the air, then shakes violently to shed water from its feathers. Once the fish is properly oriented in its talons (the head always facing forward) the osprey flies directly back to its nest or a favorite feeding perch. I was fortu-

nate to observe the same bird for a few days previous, and took note of the tree snag it kept returning to to eat its catch. Concealed in some waterside brush, I waited and lucked out as the osprey kept to its habits!

Osprey perched with a recently caught fish

NORTHERN HARRIER

Circus cyaneus

A male northern harrier in flight

The Northern Harrier is a raptor of marshes, wetlands, prairies and coastlines. Of all North American hawks, it is the most at home on or near the ground.

APPEARANCE

Length 18 inches. Wingspan 43 inches. It is a slender bird, well adapted for its role as an open-country predator. Males are much smaller than females and have a light gray head and back and brownish spots on whitish underparts. The male's wings are largely white underneath with black wing tips. The female has a brown head and back with buff-colored undersides accented with dark spots. Both sexes have a round, owl-like facial disk and long tail.

The range of the northern harrier

HABITAT

Marshes (they were formerly called marsh hawks), salt marshes, wet meadows, bogs, sloughs, prairies and savanna.

BEHAVIOR

They are buoyant and graceful in flight as they flap and glide close to the ground with wings held in a shallow "V" position while gliding. While flight hunting, the bird's head is tilted downwards to best utilize its extremely acute eyesight and hearing to zero in on its prey. During breeding season the female will fly up from the nest to meet the approaching male. He will drop the prey, which she catches in midair before returning to the nest.

Has a low tolerance of humans and will viciously protect the area surrounding the nest. Occasionally attacks larger birds such as red-tailed hawks, ravens and bald eagles if they get too close to the nest, and will routinely put the run on crows, grackles and blackbirds.

CALLS

The typical call is a series of about ten or so shrieking abrupt whistles, *kee-kee-kee-kee-kee-kee*.

The reddish-brown plumage is a characteristic of a young northern harrier

FOOD
Eats just about anything that is small enough to catch. Rodents are preferred, but snakes, frogs, rabbits, squirrels, grasshoppers and dragonflies are also prey. American bitterns, ducks, green herons and smaller species of birds are occasionally taken.

FAMILY LIFE
The only hawk species in North America that nests on the ground. The flimsy nest of sticks and coarse grasses is from 16–31 inches in diameter and about 2 inches in height, higher in wet areas.

Generally five eggs are incubated exclusively by the female for approximately 31 or 32 days. Young are fed by both parents and after about 35 days they are ready to fly. Afterwards, they remain around the nest for a few weeks. During this time the parents teach them how to hunt. One brood per year.

MIGRATION
Migrating birds usually arrive on their breeding grounds from March to mid-May. Fall migration runs from mid-August to late October (some birds linger until November). Is year-round resident over much of the southern part of its range, and individuals will occasionally winter in northern breeding areas.

CONSERVATION CONCERNS
Species status overall in North America is secure with stable or declining population. Is locally vulnerable to extinction in over twenty U.S. states. Thought to be declining throughout most of its range due to habitat loss.

RELATED SPECIES
Is the only North American harrier species.

A conservation status map of the northern harrier

RED-SHOULDERED HAWK

Buteo lineatus

Red-shouldered hawks are one of the most common hawk species found in wooded wetlands throughout eastern North America

The red-shouldered hawk is often the most common hawk in its habitat. Here it will be found haunting its favorite swamps and wooded wetlands as it waits to swoop on unsuspecting prey.

APPEARANCE

Length 17 inches. Wingspan 40 inches. A fairly large hawk, somewhat smaller and less robust than a red-tailed hawk. Reddish shoulders, breast heavily barred in rusty red, with yellow legs and feet. The cere (the area around the nostrils at the base of the bill) is a bright yellow. Black-and-white checkered flight feathers. In flight look for the narrow white banding on the long tail as well as short, abrupt wing beats. From below a translucent, finely barred crescent just before the wing's primary feathers is unmistakable.

HABITAT

Favored habitats include swamps, wooded wetlands, riparian forests and river bottoms.

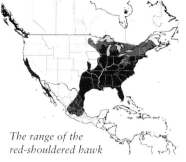

The range of the red-shouldered hawk

BEHAVIOR

Unlike many of the other *Buteo* species, which tend to soar while hunting, the red-shouldered hawk is more sedentary, soaring less frequently, and usually hunting from a low perch. Here it waits patiently for some unsuspecting prey to happen by, then drops down to capture it. In flight it may be seen soaring beautifully on wide outstretched wings and a broad, fanned tail, or gliding low over a marsh in search of prey.

CALLS

A clearly uttered, powerful drawn-out *kee-yah*, *kee-yah* is repeated.

FOOD

A very broad diet includes small mammals, snakes, reptiles, frogs, snails, spiders, earthworms, crayfish, caterpillars and occasionally birds.

FAMILY LIFE

The nest is placed in a tree, usually on a large branch close to the trunk at a height of 23–66 feet. It is made of sticks, twigs, strips of bark, leaves or moss and is lined with green leaves and other plant matter. Generally, three eggs are incubated by both adults for 28 days. The young are fed by both parents for about 39 to 45 days until the young can fly. Red-shouldered hawk pairs or their offspring may use the same nesting territory for decades.

MIGRATION

Is migratory only in the northern portion of its breeding range. Spring birds generally arrive very early on the breeding grounds, usually in late February and March and will leave on southward migration in October or November.

CONSERVATION CONCERNS

Species status overall in North America is secure and the population is stable or increasing. In Canada it is a species of special concern due to its limited range. Like all species of hawks, the red-shouldered was persecuted well into the twentieth century. Formerly known as the "hen hawk," it was wrongly thought to prey heavily on chickens and so was heavily hunted. Habitat loss also caused a decline in its numbers. The population appears to be stable, but ongoing destruction of its habitat and pollution pose a continued threat.

RELATED SPECIES

The red-shouldered hawk belongs to the genus *Buteo*, of which there are eight other regularly occurring species in North America.

A red-shouldered hawk perched low in a tree over a swamp

BALD EAGLE

Haliaeetus leucocephalus

The bald eagle is the top avian predator in the wetland

One of the largest and most recognizable birds in North America, the bald eagle is at the top of the avian food chain.

APPEARANCE
Length 31 inches. Wingspan 80 inches. It is the largest bird of prey in North America. Adults are dark brown with a white head, neck and tail. The bill and feet are yellow. It takes about four years for the pure white head and tail to be acquired. Immature birds are mottled brown.

HABITAT
Is generally found near water. Breeds and hunts in the vicinity of lakes, rivers and coasts. Often found in wetlands where there is a large concentration of waterfowl.

BEHAVIOR

The bald eagle is a versatile forager. Hunts fish by snatching them from the surface of the water. In the west it scavenges salmon that are dead or dying after spawning, and also pirates fish from ospreys. Preys on seabird colonies in northern coastal areas. Small mammals such as muskrats are also taken. Immatures and adults congregate at wetlands and coastal bays where there are large concentrations of migrating waterfowl to hunt wounded birds. Also scavenges dead animals. Adults are unmistakable in flight. Has a very slow wing beat and a steady moderate flight and will often soar.

The range of the bald eagle

CALLS

Call is a weak, squeaky and repetitive *kik-kik-kik*.

FOOD

Diet includes primarily fish, but also small mammals, birds and carrion.

FAMILY LIFE

Both adults build an extremely large platform nest of various size sticks and plants, lined with a variety of material, generally built in the top of a large tree overlooking the water. Both adults incubate the two eggs for 34 to 36 days. Young are fed by both adults. First flight at 70 to 98 days.

MIGRATION

Is migratory over the northern part of its range where it arrives in early spring, and leaves after young are fledged, often stopping for extended periods at areas of high food concentration on its way south.

CONSERVATION CONCERNS

Species status overall in North America is secure and growing. Formerly listed as an *endangered* species, now upgraded to a federally threatened species in United States as a result of the species' success. Decimated by hunting in the nineteenth and early twentieth centuries and by DDT in the mid-twentieth century, the bald eagle's population

A conservation status map of the bald eagle

was reduced drastically to such a low point that its extinction was feared. Fortunately, its population has rebounded significantly since the late 1970s with numbers doubling every 6 to 7 years.

RELATED SPECIES

The only other eagle that breeds in North America is the golden eagle.

An immature bald eagle

PEREGRINE FALCON

Falco peregrinus

A perching peregrine falcon shows off its large, powerful feet

Formerly called the duck hawk (though it is not a member of the hawk family) for its penchant for hunting wetland birds, the peregrine falcon is one of the most spectacular and efficient avian hunters on the planet.

APPEARANCE

Length 16 inches. Wingspan 41 inches. This sleek, powerful bird of prey, about the size of a crow, has a slate-gray back and head. The very large, yellow feet are noticeable when the bird is perching. Has a yellow ring around the very large, dark eyes and around the base of the bill, a dark "moustache" under the eyes, the throat and upper breast are white or buff and the belly generally has dark barring. In flight, the peregrine has a rapid, shallow wing beat and its long, pointed wings and fairly short tail are apparent.

The female is noticeably larger than the male.

HABITAT
Generally found near water, they favor coastal areas, where they prey on birds in salt marshes, beaches, barrier islands, estuaries, mudflats and even open ocean. They also frequent freshwater marshes.

The range of the peregrine falcon

BEHAVIOR
The peregrine falcon specializes in hunting small to medium-sized birds, which it generally captures by diving (called "stooping") at them from above at tremendous speeds of up to 175 miles an hour. Birds are usually killed in midair by a blow from the falcon's large and powerful feet. Will also pursue birds in rapid level flight, often along a beach, over mudflats or open water. Birds that are knocked out of the air are later retrieved on the ground. Mated pairs often hunt cooperatively. Will "play" by harassing hawks, egrets, herons and flocks of smaller species without any intent of killing them. I once watched a particularily bold falcon dive-bomb a terrified barn cat in the middle of a cow pasture.

CALLS
Seldom heard, the call is a harsh *kek-kek-kek*.

FOOD
Diet is almost exclusively birds, from small songbirds to large ducks. In wetland areas, sandpipers, plovers and waterfowl are an important part of its diet.

FAMILY LIFE
The female scrapes a crude nest generally high on a cliff ledge that is protected by an overhang of rock or vegetation. The nest site often has a commanding view of the surrounding landscape or the

sea. Rarely, they will use an old tree nest or tree cavity and will occasionally nest on the ledge of a skyscraper. They return to the nest year after year. Generally three or four eggs are incubated by both adults for 29 to 32 days. Both parents feed the young until they leave the nest after 35 to 42 days.

MIGRATION
Has the widest distribution of any bird on earth, and is found on all continents except Antarctica. West Coast and extreme south-western birds are year-round residents, while Artic and other North American populations are generally migratory.

CONSERVATION CONCERNS
Species status overall in North America is apparently secure and stable. Is listed as an endangered species in the United States and a threatened species in Canada. In the early 1990s, populations were estimated at only several thousand breeding pairs across North America. In the twentieth century the widespread use of DDT resulted in a population crash and it was extirpated from many parts of its range. The regulation of DDT use and captive-breeding programs that release birds back into the wild has resulted in a slow but steady come-back of the species. Destruction of wetland habitats, which its primary prey species rely on, still threaten the health of its population.

A conservation status map of the peregrine falcon

RELATED SPECIES
The peregrine falcon is one of six species of falcons in North America. They all belong to the genus *Falco*.

SHORT-EARED OWL

Asio flammeus

Hunting by sight as well as sound, the short-eared owl has some of the most acute eyes and ears of the avian world

The short-eared owl can frequently be seen flying buoyantly along in the daytime as it hunts freshwater and saltwater marshes and surrounding grasslands. Although it shares habitats with the more common northern harrier, the deep flapping of the short-eared owl's wings and its irregular flight readily distinguishes it from the similar-sized hawk at a distance.

APPEARANCE
Length 15 inches. Wingspan 38 inches. A medium-sized owl with tawny or buff-brown plumage and streaked underparts. The large head and short neck give the bird a decidedly blunt appearance, especially in flight. The "ear" tufts are small and difficult to see. Defined facial disk with bright yellow eyes, each surrounded by a dark triangle. A dark "wrist patch" is visible on the underside of

141

The range of the short-eared owl

the wings. Males are somewhat lighter overall than females.

HABITAT
Freshwater marshes, salt marshes, meadows, dunes, upland fields, prairies, tundra and savanna.

BEHAVIOR
The short-eared owl hunts during the day and night by flying low back and forth over marshes and fields where rodents are abundant. Occasionally circles and hovers. It will extend its feet and drop quickly to the ground to capture prey. Often perches on a post or low tree to watch for prey. Will gather in relatively large numbers in areas where there is a cyclical abundance of prey such as voles or field mice.

Unlike most owls, short-eared owls hunt during daylight hours, especially at dusk and in the pre-sunrise dawn as this one is doing

CALLS

Silent except on its breeding grounds where a variety of sounds are made including a loud, high-pitched *yak-yak-yak, yak-yak-yak* like the sound of a small barking dog or the male's *too-too-too-too* in a rapid series.

FOOD

Rodents such as voles, mice and rats are favored, but occasionally takes birds and large insects such as grasshoppers and beetles.

FAMILY LIFE

Nests on the ground. In a marsh or field, the female builds a nest lined with grasses, weed stems and feathers in a shallow depression, usually concealed by surrounding grass (on very rare occasions may nest in a burrow in the ground). Generally four to seven eggs are laid which are incubated exclusively by the female for 24 to 28 days. During incubation she is fed by the male. Both parents feed

A short-eared owl hunting low cocks its head toward the sound of a rodent in the grass

the newly hatched young until they fledge at 31 to 36 days. In areas where prey is abundant, several nests may be found within the same proximity. One brood per year.

MIGRATION
Migrating birds usually arrive on their northern breeding grounds from late March to early May. Fall migration generally takes place between mid-September to November. Birds throughout the great plains to the West Coast of the United States and Canada's southern prairies are non-migratory.

CONSERVATION CONCERNS
Species status overall in North America is secure but declining in the United States, and vulnerable in Canada, where it is officially listed as a "species of special concern." In certain areas, such as the northeastern United States and Canada's maritime provinces, it is quite rare. Still relatively common on the American plains and southern Canadian prairies. The greatest cause of decline through-out the continent is habitat loss due to the destruction of wetlands, grasslands and coastal areas preferred by the birds.

RELATED SPECIES
The short-eared owl is one of eighteen North American species in the family *Strigidae*, or "typical" owls.

RAILS

CLAPPER RAIL

Rallis longirostris

The elusive clapper rail wading at the edge of a brackish marsh

Although its clattering call is often heard, the drab clapper rail (or marsh hen as it was formerly called) is rarely seen as it goes about its business on the salt marsh.

APPEARANCE
Length 14 inches. Wingspan 19 inches. This large, overall drab olive-brown rail has a long, slightly down-curved bill and husky grayish-yellow legs.

HABITAT
Prefers salt marshes, but also brackish areas, mangroves and, occasionally, freshwater marshes.

The range of the clapper rail

BEHAVIOR

Usually forages on open mud-flats and along the banks of marsh creeks during low tide. Walks with long strides, bobbing its head, twitching its tail and pecking the ground for food. An adept swimmer, it will dive to avoid predators, often staying underwater with only the bill and nostrils protruding so it can breathe until the danger has passed. Is very swift on foot when fleeing danger, passing easily through tangled underbrush and able to squeeze through extremely narrow passages between the stems of vegetation, hence the term "thin as a rail." When flushed, its flight is weak and awkward and it often moves toward the thing that threatens it. This is one of the reasons they were so efficiently slaughtered by hunters early in the twentieth century.

CALLS

Extremely loud, staccato *kek kek kek* call given in rapid succession of about two per second. Calls most actively at dusk, but also during both day and night. Just one alarming noise will set off a protesting chorus of dozens of clapper rails across the marsh.

FOOD

Crabs and other crustaceans, snails, mussels and marine worms.

FAMILY LIFE

Both sexes participate in building the nest, which is usually a cupped mass of stems, grass and tidal detritus, sometimes dome-shaped, and located on a marsh or stream bank; occasionally concealed under a bush. Generally seven to eleven eggs are incubated by both adults for 20 to 23 days. Both sexes tend the young for about 40 days and they make their first flight after 63 to 70 days. One or two broods annually.

MIGRATION

Birds in the southern part of their range are year-round, nonmigratory residents. Birds that breed to the north generally winter in the coastal regions of the southeastern Atlantic and southern Pacific North America and southward.

CONSERVATION CONCERNS

Species status overall in North America is secure and stable in the United States. However, the Yuma clapper rail, a subspecies, is listed as endangered.

RELATED SPECIES

There are eight other species of rail in North America, including the sora, black rail, yellow rail, king rail, Virginia rail, purple gallinule, common moorhen and the American coot.

RAILS

A clapper rail foraging in a brackish marsh

SORA

Porzana carolina

*The sora uses its large feet to support itself on top of floating,
decaying vegetation*

More often heard than seen, the sora is one of the most widespread
wetland birds in all of North America.

APPEARANCE
Length 8–9 inches. Wingspan 14 inches. Roughly the size of a
plump robin, it has a stubby tail, long yellow legs and a yellow,
chicken-like bill. Is generally brown with some black streaking and
a grayish breast. The throat and front of face are black and the eye
is bright red. Very large feet are adapted for walking across
floating vegetation.

HABITAT
Generally freshwater marshes with heavy vegetation.

BEHAVIOR

Secretive by nature, preferring the cover of dense cattail or reed growth. Treads along floating vegetation while gleaning food. Is known to swim both on the surface and underwater to evade predators. Naturalist C.J. Maynard wrote: "I once saw one run nimbly along the bottom

The range of the sora

of a brook, the water of which was about a foot deep, by clinging to aquatic plants it emerged on the other side, thus passing over some 15 feet while submerged."

CALLS

A number of distinctive calls, but none more so than the bizarre, horse-like whinny call, which consists of about a dozen short, clear whistles in a rapidly descending scale, followed by three or more notes on an even pitch. Other calls include the more commonly heard repetitive *er-wee er-wee*, a sweet, plaintive song that is usually heard in spring.

FOOD

The seeds of marsh plants are the most important food source, but aquatic snails, insects, insect larvae and possibly tadpoles and leeches are also taken.

FAMILY LIFE

Male and female build a 6-inch diameter basket-shaped nest of woven cattail blades, grasses or rushes, carefully lined with fine materials and placed among the heavy cover of overarching vegetation. Ten to twelve eggs are incubated by both parents for about 19 days. The newly hatched leave the nest and can swim almost immediately. The young are fed by the parents for about 3 weeks until their first flight. Two broods per year.

MIGRATION

Generally arrives on its breeding marshes in March to May. Fall migration is generally from late August to October. Is year-round nonmigratory resident in parts of New Mexico and coastal California.

CONSERVATION CONCERNS

Species status overall in North America is secure but declining. Because it is a small, secretive bird, its actual numbers are difficult

to determine. Unlike some of its sister species in the rail family, the sora is still relatively abundant, but its population appears to be declining, particularly in central North America. Much of its preferred habitat is threatened in the United States.

A conservation status map of the sora

RELATED SPECIES

Soras belong to the rail family, which includes eight other North American species.

Photographer's Journal

A robin-sized sora treads lightly across floating vegetation as it searches for food. For years I had heard the bizarre, horse-like whinny call of the sora, but never saw one. I knew that this rarely seen bird was very secretive and spent much of its time in the deep recesses of the marsh, under the cover of thick cattails. Cryptic coloring and slow, deliberate movement only added to the difficulty of finding a sora, but I set out to do just that. I decided the best approach was to listen for its call and try homing in on it. This is easier said than done, since several soras may be calling at different spots in the marsh, making pinpointing the sound difficult. However, after a few days of looking, I spotted one along the edge of some cattails. Moving slowly in my floating blind, I was able to get within just a few feet of the bird. To my surprise, the bird slowly submerged like a submarine, only to surface about 15 feet away. (Apparently, the birds actually walk underwater, keeping themselves down by holding onto vegetation!) Once it got used to the blind, the bird completely ignored me. I also learned that a sora's whinny call is quite ear-splitting when it's just a few feet away!

A sora forages on vegetation, its large feet plainly visible

COMMON MOORHEN

Gallinula chloropus

The common moorhen is a quite beautiful marsh bird

At a distance the common moorhen looks like a duck on the water, but get closer and you'll notice its small, distinctly un-duck-like bill, and the fact that its head continually bobs as it swims.

APPEARANCE
Length 14 inches. Wingspan 21 inches. About the size of a green-winged teal, dark overall, and the brownish-olive green back and charcoal gray underparts are separated from one another by a white line on the side. It has a black head and neck, bright red bill with a yellow tip and yellow legs with large feet.

HABITAT
Freshwater marshes with an abundance of vegetation and some open water. Also inhabits heavy vegetated areas along the edges of

ponds, lakes and slow-moving streams.

BEHAVIOR
Can be quite tame and approach-able. Forages by walking through the marsh across floating vegetation while pecking food from the cattails, other plants and off the water with its small

The range of the common moorhen

bill. Walks with a jerking, flicking movement of the tail and swims by pumping its head back and forth while it paddles with its large, unwebbed feet.

CALLS
One of the noisiest birds of the wetlands, it is constantly vocalizing with others of its kind. Gives a host of chicken-like clucks, as well as a series of loud squawks, followed by a clipped *kup-kup-kup-kup*.

FOOD
Diet includes aquatic and terrestrial insects, worms, mollusks such as snails, aquatic vegetation, berries and seeds.

FAMILY LIFE
Are often in loose colonies. Both adults build a shallow cup-shaped nest of dead and dried aquatic vegetation lined with grasses, usually placed on a hummock of dead cattails or other plant material. Will often build more than one nest platform, but will use only one. The usual five to eight eggs are incubated for 19 to 22 days by both parents. The young are fed by both adults (as well as by nonbreeding birds) for 40 to 50 days until they are able to fly. One to three broods annually.

MIGRATION
Usually begins to arrive on its breeding grounds during late March to May (later in northern areas) and generally migrates south

RAILS

throughout the fall months. Is year-round resident in the southern United States.

CONSERVATION CONCERNS
Species status overall in North America is secure and stable in the United States, and apparently secure in Canada. Declining locally in many areas due to habitat loss.

RELATED SPECIES
Is the only member of its genus *Gallinula*; part of the *Rallid* family, which also includes the American coot, the purple gallinule and the rails.

A pair of common moorhens

AMERICAN COOT

Fulica americana

American coots are plump, somewhat duck-like members of the rail family

This largest and most aquatic member of the rail family in North America is extremely widespread and quite abundant throughout much of the continent.

APPEARANCE
Length 15 inches. Wingspan 24 inches. Large, duck-sized water-bird. It is an overall slate gray with a black head and neck, and a short, white, chicken-like bill. Spends much time on the surface of the water swimming like a duck. Has stout grayish-green legs, and very large feet with lobed toes. A thin white line is conspicuous on the trailing edge of the wing when in flight. Has rapid, shallow wing beats with trailing legs in flight.

HABITAT

Freshwater lakes, ponds, rivers, marshes, occasionally in salt or brackish waters.

BEHAVIOR

Forages in the manner of a dabbling duck by tipping up to get at food in shallow water. Also dives for food to depths over 15

The range of the American coot

feet like a grebe. Is very aggressive and will often pursue other birds vigorously to chase them from the vicinity. Pirates food from ducks. Needs to vigorously run across the surface of the water to get airborne. Can form very large, dense flocks during the non-breeding season. At times, a flock can be so closely packed that it looks like a single organism as it moves across the water. Coots are also quite mobile on land and frequently feed in fields and other grassy areas.

CALLS

Most commonly heard sound is a single *krip*. A near continuous stream of grunts, croaks, quacks and clucks are heard from a flock of coots.

An American coot gathers speed for takeoff

FOOD
Largely aquatic vegetation such as grasses and algae, but will also eat fish, tadpoles, small crustaceans, worms, snails and both aquatic and terrestrial insects. Will eat grasses and waste grains on land.

FAMILY LIFE
Both sexes participate in building the nest, a large cup-shaped structure of stems and leaves that rests on a floating platform of plant material anchored to living plants over water up to 3 feet or so deep. Generally eight to twelve eggs are incubated for 21 to 25 days by both adults. Young leave the nest almost immediately and are fed by both parents until their first flight at 49 to 56 days days. One or two broods annually.

MIGRATION
Birds in the southern half of the range are year-round residents. Northerly birds generally arrive on their breeding grounds in March or April and leave on their southerly migration in October or November. Birds breed and winter as far south as Panama.

CONSERVATION CONCERNS
Species status overall in North America is secure and stable.

RELATED SPECIES
Is one of nine rail species in North America.

American coots gather in large, dense flocks during the winter

SHOREBIRDS, GULLS AND TERNS

BLACK-BELLIED PLOVER

Pluvialis squatarola

A black-bellied plover's most distinguishing marks are its black armpits, or axillar feathers

This stocky shorebird, the largest of all North American plover species, is known in Europe as the gray plover for its familiar drab plumage, which is seen during fall migration as the bird passes though temperate areas.

APPEARANCE
Length 12 inches. Wingspan 29 inches. During fall migration it is reminiscent of a very small gull with overall gray plumage mottled with dark specks on the large head and the tops of the wings. During breeding season the lower part of the head, the throat and the belly are black. In all plumages the black axillar feathers (in the armpits) are visible during flight. Sexes look similar.

The range of the black-belllied plover

HABITAT
Coastal tidal flats, sandbars, salt marshes, lakeshores, shallow grassy or muddy marshes.

BEHAVIOR
Forages in the manner of other plovers by picking food items off the ground. Is an extremely wary bird. Like virtually all shorebirds, the black-bellied plover travels and feeds in flocks of widely varying size during migration. Rarely observed on summer breeding grounds, they are easily frightened and very difficult to approach, a behavior that may have helped them weather heavy hunting pressure in the nineteenth and early twentieth centuries. On their wintering grounds they have a reputation for being quite aggressive and will vigorously defend a feeding territory against others of their flock.

Because black-bellied plovers are most commonly seen during fall migration when they are in their drab non-breeding plumage, they are known as gray plovers in the U.K. and Europe

CALLS
Most commonly heard is the flight call, a melodious whistling *pee-u-wee* with the middle note the lowest.

FOOD
Insects, earthworms, marine worms, crustaceans, mollusks and various other invertebrates are taken. Seeds are occasionally also eaten.

FAMILY LIFE
Nest is a slight hollow on the tundra, lined with

lichen, grass or moss. The male scrapes the hollow, the female lines the nest. Both sexes incubate four eggs for 26 or 27 days. The female deserts the chicks after about 12 days, and the male continues to feed them until they are fledglings at about 23 days. One brood per year.

MIGRATION
Usually arrives on its northern breeding grounds in May and June and begins breeding shortly after. Southward migration begins in July and birds are seen up until October in our more southerly areas as they stop over to feed before continuing their journey.

CONSERVATION CONCERNS
Species status overall in North America is secure in the U.S. and apparently secure in Canada. The population possibly declining in Canada. Still quite common in North America with an estimated population of 200,000. May have been very abundant before they were commercially hunted during the nineteenth century. Habitat loss in their wintering range in South America may pose a future threat.

RELATED SPECIES
Its closest relative is the quite similar American golden plover of the same genus *Pluvialis*.

Did You Know?
Wetland birds perform some the greatest migratory feats in the animal world. The black-bellied plover migrates from nesting grounds in the high Arctic to wintering areas near the southern tip of South America, a distance of 8,700 miles, one way. In six days a banded lesser yellowlegs flew nonstop from Massachusetts to Martinique in the Caribbean, a distance of 2,000 miles. Sandhill cranes migrate up to 4,350 miles one way from breeding areas in the high Arctic and Siberia to wintering areas in southern Canada and the United States.

KILLDEER

Charadrius vociferus

A killdeer on the shore

The scientific species name, *vociferus*, says it all: The killdeer is one of the most vocal of all the shorebirds. Its grating call, begun at the slightest approach, is unmistakable and is usually heard before the bird is seen.

APPEARANCE
Length 11 inches. Wingspan 24 inches. It is the largest of the *Charadrius* or ringed plovers as they are known. Brownish-gray upperparts, white underparts, two distinctive black breast bands, rufous orange rump, a long tail (most obvious in flight), pinkish legs and feet and a very noticeable red eye-ring distinguish the killdeer.

HABITAT
Live in almost any relatively open area—mudflats, wet pastures,

ditches, gravel pits, upland fields, meadows, the margins of fresh-water marshes, ponds, streams and golf courses. Occasionally found in coastal areas along lagoons and mudflats.

BEHAVIOR

The range of the killdeer

Feeds by running, stopping and looking, then pecking prey off the ground both in wetland environments and drier upland habitats. Despite its loud vocal protestations, it has become comfortable living in close proximity with humans. This widespread and adaptable bird has benefited greatly from human development of the landscape where grassy and open areas are created. Feigns injury to draw potential predators away from its nest.

CALLS

Is very vocal. Has numerous calls, but the most commonly heard one is a loud and rapidly repeated *kill-dee kill-dee kill-dee.*

FOOD

Mostly insects, also a variety of other invertebrates.

FAMILY LIFE

The male builds the nest, a scraped out depression on an elevated piece of ground (if available) usually in a pasture, a gravel pit or other open area, often near human habitation. Generally four eggs are incubated by both sexes for 24 to 28 days. Young leave the nest and feed themselves soon after hatching but are tended by both adults for 25 days until they can fly. Two broods annually.

MIGRATION

Resident year round in much of the United States and the West Coast of Canada. More northerly breeding birds are one of the first species to arrive on the breeding grounds in February and March, often arriving at the same time as the American robin and considered by many as a harbinger of spring. Fall migration from northern areas generally begins in late summer and continues until late fall.

CONSERVATION CONCERNS
Species status overall in North America is secure and stable in the United States and Canada. Worldwide population is estimated at 1 million.

RELATED SPECIES
Is one of six plovers in the genus *Charadrius* that regularly breed in North America, which also includes the Wilson's, snowy, semi-palmated, piping and the rare common ringed plover.

The killdeer is the largest of the "ringed" plovers

SEMI-PALMATED PLOVER

Charadrius semipalmatus

Semi-palmated plover on the beach

The semi-palmated plover, named for the partial webbing between its toes, is a widespread migrant throughout North America. It is most often seen running along beaches in the late summer and fall.

APPEARANCE
Length 7 inches. Wingspan 19 inches. It is the size of a robin and the upperparts are brown, the color of wet sand. The rather large eyes are surrounded by a distinctive black mask and the bill is orange with a black tip, but is completely black in winter. A single thick black band rings the lower neck. The throat, the side of the neck and underparts are white and the legs are orange. Sexes look similar.

The range of the semi-palmated plover

HABITAT

Both fresh and saltwater mud-flats, shallow marshes, beaches, shores of river mouths, lakes, ponds, and flooded fields. Freshwater habitats are used more commonly during migration. Nests on grassy tundra, gravel bars and beaches.

BEHAVIOR

Travels in loose flocks, often associating with other plover and sandpiper species during migration. A very active forager that runs rapidly with head held high. Looks and listens intently for prey item before picking it up. Flocks scatter widely during feeding. After foraging at low tide along a beach, flocks pack together to rest on the upper beach when the tide comes in.

CALLS

Common calls include a clear *pee-wit* or *cher-wee*. A less common call is an odd *whinny* that is occasionally heard during migration.

FOOD

Semi-palmated plovers eat small mollusks, marine worms and crustaceans in the marine environment and aquatic insects and worms in freshwater areas.

FAMILY LIFE

The nest, built by the male, is a depression in gravel, sand, moss and sometimes in dead seaweed; occasionally lightly lined with grasses, pebbles or broken shells. Both sexes incubate the four eggs for about 24 days. The young leave the nest very soon after hatching and begin feeding themselves almost immediately, though they continue to be tended by the adults. First flight occurs at 22 to 31 days. One brood per year.

MIGRATION
Is usually seen during spring migration in May. Begins breeding in early June. Fall migrants are seen as early as July and will remain on migration until late September and sometimes later.

CONSERVATION CONCERNS
Species status overall in North America is secure and the population is stable. Is common in places during migration. However, its numbers are likely much lower now than they were prior to the late nineteenth century when they were decimated by hunting.

RELATED SPECIES
The semi-palmated plover's closest relatives are the five other species belonging to the genus *Charadrius*: the killdeer, and ringed, Wilson's, snowy, mountain and the endangered piping plovers.

A semi-palmated plover resting on a freshwater mudflat during fall migration

PIPING PLOVER
Charadrius melodus

Piping plovers blend well with their surroundings

This charming little bird, so well camouflaged and inconspicuous in its sandy nesting habitat, has attracted much attention from conservationists because of its very low population and limited range in North America.

APPEARANCE
Length 7 inches. Wingspan 19 inches. A small, stocky plover, overall pale sandy gray with a black necklace (often missing in winter plumage), white forehead and lores and, short yellowish-orange legs. Stout bill is orange with a black tip during breeding season, but blackish-orange during the rest of the year. Has large, black eyes and white underparts.

HABITAT

Both freshwater (the Great Lakes region) and saltwater (the Atlantic Coast) habitats are utilized, as well as mostly sandy and pebbly beaches (especially those with broad, flat areas above the high-tide mark) and dunes, particularly those with scattered bunches of grass. Feeds along the edges of mud-flats on the coast, and the edges of ponds, marshes and lakes.

The range of the piping plover

BEHAVIOR

This small plover is so well adapted to its surroundings that in sandy environments it is practically invisible until it moves. In typical plover style, it forages by running along the wet sand or on the mud, stopping suddenly, eyeing the ground beneath, then picking up its prey. Often escapes predators by running very quickly along the sand, stopping suddenly and crouching motionless. Will feign injury to draw predators away from its nest.

CALLS

The piping plover's call is a soft, flute-like *peep-lo*. Also gives a series of clear whistles.

FOOD

Marine worms, insect larvae, beetles, crustaceans, mollusks and marine invertebrate eggs.

FAMILY LIFE

Is normally a solitary nester, but will also breed in loose colonies where numbers permit (which, given its sparse population, is not often). Both sexes build the nest, a scrape in the sand or gravel, lined with bits of shells, driftwood and pebbles to help conceal it. The nest is built high up on the beach, well above the high water

A piping plover, one of the endangered wetland birds in North America

line. Four eggs are incubated by both sexes for 21 to 31 days. The young are tended and fed by both parents for 20 to 35 days until they make their first flight. One brood annually.

MIGRATION

Generally arrives on its breeding grounds between late March and mid-April and leaves on its southerly migration between early August and late September.

CONSERVATION CONCERNS

Species status overall in North America is endangered or threatened (depending on the area) in the United States, and is endangered in Canada. Hunting drove the piping plover almost to extinction in the late nineteenth and early twentieth centuries. Development of its limited nesting habitat (both around the Great Lakes and on the Atlantic Coast) and continued disturbance of the bird by humans during nesting season continue to be serious challenges to its survival.

A conservation status map of the piping plover

RELATED SPECIES

Is one of six plovers in the genus *Charadrius* that regularly breed in North America, which also includes the killdeer, snowy, semi-palmated, Wilson's and rare common ringed plovers.

SNOWY PLOVER

Charadrius alexandrinus

Snowy plovers are the smallest species of plover

This smallest of the North American plovers is not easily distinguished from its larger cousin, the piping plover, particularly in winter.

APPEARANCE
Length 6 inches. Wingspan 17 inches. This very small plover is whiter overall than its sister species. It is very pale above with white under-parts, a small, relatively slender black bill, slate-gray legs and a dark (darker during breeding season) eye line. Males have a heavier, darker breast mark or band than females.

HABITAT
Beaches, mudflats, evaporated salt or alkaline flats that are located inland, sandy margins of rivers and streams, lakes and ponds.

The range of the snowy plover

BEHAVIOR

Forages either along the edge of water or on the flats like other small plovers by running along and pecking food items. Picks among detritus and sea wrack on the beach for flies and other invertebrates. Also uses a "pattering" technique where it vibrates its foot on the ground to draw out prey.

CALLS

Flight call is an abrupt *kweep* or husky *koor-wij*.

FOOD

Insects, crustaceans, mollusks, worms, tiny fish and other invertebrates.

FAMILY LIFE

Often nests in loose colonies near least tern colonies. The male builds the nest, a scrape in the sand or gravel on an elevated area of a

This snowy plover male has been leg-banded by biologists who are studying the species

beach or other flat area, lined with bits of twigs, shells, driftwood and pebbles to help conceal it; often located near a tuft of grass. Generally three eggs are incubated by both sexes for 25 to 32 days. Young are fed by both parents for 31 days until they can fly. One brood in the east, often two broods in the western part of its range.

MIGRATION

This is a very wide-ranging species that breeds on every continent. Populations in the extreme coastal United States are resident year round. Inland populations to the west (including a small population in Saskatchewan) migrate south during the winter.

CONSERVATION CONCERNS

Species status overall in North America is vulnerable in the United States (considered threatened in the western United States); imperiled in Canada where a small breeding population is limited to a few places in southern Saskatchewan.

RELATED SPECIES

Is one of six plovers in the genus *Charadrius* that regularly breed in North America, which also includes the killdeer, piping plover, semipalmated plover, Wilson's plover and rare common ringed plover.

A conservation status map of the snowy plover

WILSON'S PLOVER

Charadruis wilsonia

A Wilson's plover feeding in the mudflats edging a salt marsh

This largely coastal species has one of the most restricted ranges of any species of plover. However, it is one of the most common small plovers in its wintering habitat, where it is often found with snowy and piping plovers.

APPEARANCE
Length 8 inches. Wingspan 19 inches. This is a small shorebird with a dark brown upperparts, a blackish neck band, white underparts, large black eyes and pinkish flesh-tone legs. The dark crowned head and heavy black bill are noticeably larger than those other small plovers.

HABITAT
Sandy beaches, sandbars, tidal mudflats and pools, and the edges

of lagoons, usually near the coast.

BEHAVIOR

Forages in a manner similar to other small plovers by walking or running along the beach or mud and picking prey from the ground. Will often run quickly down the beach to flee danger

The range of the Wilson's plover

rather than take flight. Flight is very fast on quick-beating wings. Will perform a distraction display by feigning injury to draw potential predators away from its nest.

CALLS

An abrupt whistled *queet*.

FOOD

Small crabs, other crustaceans, sand worms, insects and small mollusks.

FAMILY LIFE

Nests in loose colonies, occasionally in the proximity of terns and oystercatchers. The male scrapes a shallow depression in sand or gravel above the tide line amid concealing shells, pebbles, plants stems or driftwood, usually placed near an object such as a tuft of grass. Generally three eggs are incubated for 23 or 24 days by both sexes. Young are fed by both parents for 21 days until they can fly. One brood annually.

MIGRATION

Less migratory than other small North American plovers. Birds in the northern part of the breeding range migrate to the coastal southern United States during the winter. Most southern birds are resident year round.

CONSERVATION CONCERNS

Overall species status in North America is apparently secure and stable in the United States. Its limited range, while often using development-prone beaches and its small North American population of an estimated 6,000 birds, should be cause for concern.

RELATED SPECIES

Is one of six plovers in the genus *Charadrius* that regularly breed in North America, which also includes the killdeer, and snowy, semi-palmated, piping and rare common ringed plovers.

Wilson's plover are distinguished from their close relatives by the large, heavy bill

AMERICAN OYSTERCATCHER

Haematopus palliatus

The striking American oystercatcher is one of the most boldly colored of all wetland species

This striking shorebird, with its clownish appearance, large blood red bill and chunky size stands out boldly from the rather drab plovers and sandpipers it associates with.

APPEARANCE
Length 17 inches. Wingspan 32 inches. A large, heavy-set shorebird, with a black head and neck, dark brown back, white underparts, distinctive bright red, long and laterally compressed bill, yellow eye with bright red eye-ring and pale legs. Bold white wing stripe is conspicuous in flight.

HABITAT
Coastal beaches, mudflats, lagoons, rocky shorelines, islands and other saltwater wetlands; seldom found inland.

The range of the American oystercatcher

BEHAVIOR

Is usually solitary or in small groups. Forages by inserting its bill (which is triangular in cross-section, making it very rigid) into bivalve shellfish such as oysters to partly open the shell, then severs the adductor muscle that holds the two halves together. This is one of the most complex feeding rituals among wetland birds. Young oystercatchers are fed by adults for an extended period because they require a long apprenticeship of watching the adults to learn the technique. Also feeds more traditionally on other types of prey by pecking.

CALLS

Gives an insistent, piercing *wheep wheep wheep* call when disturbed. A loud *krik krik krik* is given when it takes wing.

FOOD

Eats largely bivalves such as oysters, clams and mussels. Also takes crabs, marine worms, urchins and occasionally fish.

FAMILY LIFE

Is a solitary breeder, occasionally in loose colonies. Both sexes build the nest, which is merely a shallow depression, sometimes with a few bits of shell as a lining, located on a relatively elevated area on an upper part of the beach or other area with soft sand or gravel and is often located amid clumps of vegetation, pebbles and broken shells. Generally three eggs are incubated by both adults for 24 to 29 days. Young leave the nest shortly after hatching and are tended by both parents for 35 or more days until their first flight. One brood annually.

MIGRATION

Is generally a year-round resident throughout most of its range. Birds breeding in more northerly areas migrate.

CONSERVATION CONCERNS

Species status overall in North America is secure and stable. The North American population is approximately 9,000. Oystercatchers were brought almost to extinction due to hunting in the late nineteenth and early twentieth centuries, resulting in a range contraction from former breeding areas in the Northeast. In the 1800s John James Audubon reported that they bred as far north as Labrador. Happily, it appears the population is growing slowly and expanding northward once again, reaching Massachusetts.

RELATED SPECIES

The black oystercatcher belongs to the same genus *Haematopus*.

The American oystercatcher's bill is specially adapted for prying open bivalve shellfish

AMERICAN AVOCET

Recurvirostra americana

The American avocet, this one in winter plumage, is one of the largest shorebird species found in wetlands

The avocet is unmistakable for its very large size and bold black-and-white plumage.

APPEARANCE

Length 18 inches. Wingspan 31 inches. It is a very large shorebird that is very light overall with white underbelly and back, a light gray head and neck (head and neck are buffy brown during breeding season), black-and-white wings and very long gray legs. The very long, thin, upturned bill is unlike that of any other North American bird. In flight it extends its neck and trails its legs.

HABITAT

Marshes (occasionally shallow pools in salt marshes where it winters in the east), wet meadows, mudflats, ponds, estuaries, brackish pools and alkaline lakes.

BEHAVIOR

Is usually seen in small, tight flocks. Forages by walking or running through shallow water and sweeping its bill from side to side over the mud bottom to find food by feel. Birds often

The range of the American avocet

line up abreast and feed communally as they advance through the water. Occasionally will swim and tip up to feed like a dabbling duck. Is very inquisitive and aggressive, often flying out to meet intruders on its breeding grounds, announcing its presence with noisy protest. During nonbreeding season they are quite tame and quiet. Flight is very strong and direct.

CALLS

A loud, single *kweep* is most commonly heard.

FOOD

Largely crustaceans, but also insects, other invertebrates, and some seeds and aquatic vegetation.

FAMILY LIFE

Both sexes participate in building a nest among clumps of vegetation or in the open on sand, gravel, a mudflat or marshy ground near water. Nest is lightly lined with dry grass or mud, and may be added to as water levels rise. Generally four eggs are incubated by both adults for 22 to 29 days. The young leave the nest soon after hatching, and can soon feed themselves, but are tended by both parents for 28 to 35 days. One brood annually.

MIGRATION

Some birds along the California coast and the Gulf of Mexico in Texas are year-round residents and don't migrate. The rest of the population arrives on its breeding grounds between late March and early May and begins its southerly migration in late summer and early fall.

CONSERVATION CONCERNS
Species status overall in North America is secure and stable.

RELATED SPECIES
The only other North American species in the family *Recurvirostridae* is the black-necked stilt.

GREATER YELLOWLEGS

Tringa melanoleuca

Greater yellowlegs are distinguished from lesser yellowlegs by a longer bill relative to the head and their larger size

The greater yellowleg is a very active and noisy sandpiper that is common on inland marshes and other wet areas during migration.

APPEARANCE
Length 14 inches. Wingspan 28 inches. This long-legged, long-necked, medium-sized sandpiper is distinguished by its bright yellow legs, a bill that is longer than its head and slightly upturned, and overall slender appearance. It is mottled, dark grayish-brown overall during breeding season and paler gray during the rest of the year with whitish underparts year round. In flight the yellow feet extend beyond the tail and the white rump is apparent.

HABITAT
Shallow margins of ponds, lakes and streams, salt marshes, mudflats,

The range of the greater yelllowlegs

tide pools and shallow freshwater marshes.

BEHAVIOR

A highly alert and skittish bird, very little escapes its attention and are for this reason it is difficult to observe at close range. The body bobs up and down abruptly when the bird is alarmed. Occurs alone or in small groups, often with lesser yellowlegs. Walks and even runs quickly through the shallow water in search of food as it pecks at the water and chases little fish and invertebrates. Is often seen standing on one leg. Occasionally will swim. Flight is quite rapid. On landing, it holds its wings vertically overhead for a moment before folding them.

CALLS

Its traditional nicknames "tattler" and "yelper" are very appropriate. When alarmed, a grating three-syllable *tew-tew-tew* phrase is

A greater yellowlegs at rest and stretching

repeated over and over again. When not alarmed, a rolling series of *too-wee too-wee too-wee* is often heard.

FOOD
A wide variety of food is taken, including insects, snails, tadpoles, worms, other aquatic invertebrates, small fish and occasionally berries.

FAMILY LIFE
Nest is a scrape or depression in the ground or moss, usually on a hummock in a marsh or a bog, and lined with fine grass, moss or leaves. The four eggs are incubated for 23 days. The young fledge after 18 to 20 days. One brood per year.

MIGRATION
Migrates earlier than many shorebirds. Usually arrives on breeding grounds in either March or April and most have left on southerly migration by July or August. Spends a number of weeks at migratory stopovers feeding and fattening up before the long trip south by late October.

CONSERVATION CONCERNS
Species status overall in North America is secure and the population is stable. Probably never abundant, it is nevertheless commonly seen throughout the continent during migration. Because much of the population nests within the boreal forest below the 60th parallel, future populations may be vulnerable to increased logging pressures in these areas.

RELATED SPECIES
The very similar lesser yellowlegs is its closest relative.

LESSER YELLOWLEGS

Tringa flavipes

A lesser yellowlegs foraging in its typical habitat

This more abundant and approachable little cousin of the greater yellowlegs is often seen in mixed flocks with other shorebirds during migration.

APPEARANCE
Length 10 inches. Wingspan 24 inches. It is considerably smaller but very similar in appearance to the greater yellowlegs. The best way of distinguishing the two is by direct size comparison. Grayish brown above and whitish below. The legs tend to be a brighter, truer yellow than the greater yellowlegs and the bill is relatively shorter compared to the head. Sexes look similar.

HABITAT
Shallow margins of ponds, lakes and streams, salt marshes, mudflats,

tide pools and shallow freshwater marshes.

BEHAVIOR

Is similar to the greater yellowlegs, but is generally less
skittish and somewhat more
approachable. Forages in a similar manner, wading gracefully
through shallow water, chasing

*The range of the
lesser yellowlegs*

and picking insects and other food items from the water. Also bobs
its body up and down when alarmed. Flight is rapid and strong.

CALLS

The best way to distinguish this species from the greater yellowlegs
is by its calls. The lesser yellowlegs' flight call is a short *too-too,
too-too*, softer, lower and more clipped than the greater yellowlegs
and usually repeated with two notes instead of three or four. Tends
to be noisier when in the air.

FOOD

Prey includes aquatic and terrestrial insects, tadpoles, small crustaceans, worms and tiny fish.

FAMILY LIFE

Breeds farther north and in generally drier areas than the greater
yellowlegs. Nest is a depression on the ground, usually on high
ground or a ridge of the tundra, often some distance from water.
The four eggs are incubated for 22 or 23 days. Young fly after 18
to 20 days. One brood per year.

MIGRATION

Is often seen in migration with greater yellowlegs and other shorebirds. Spring birds generally arrive on breeding grounds in April
and May. Like its cousin, the lesser yellowlegs is usually seen at
migratory stopovers beginning in July and remain until late
October when they continue their southerly migration.

CONSERVATION CONCERNS
Species status overall in North America is secure and stable. Is relatively abundant and commonly seen during migration. Population may be up to five times that of the greater yellowlegs.

RELATED SPECIES
Greater yellowlegs and solitary sandpiper are the only two breeding species in North America sharing the same genus *Tringa*.

Frequent wing stretching is a common behavior of the lesser yellowlegs

WILLET

Catoptrophorus semipalmatus

A large shorebird, the willet is at home foraging along a costal beach as it is in a freshwater lake

One of the largest members of the sandpiper family, this rather plain bird may escape your attention at first as it rests inconspicuously on one leg near the shore.

APPEARANCE
Length 15 inches. Wingspan 26 inches. This is a large, heavy-bodied sandpiper with a fairly long neck and legs, a plumage of overall light gray, a thick gray-black bill, bluish or brownish legs and whitish underparts. During breeding season the birds are quite heavily spotted on the throat and breast. In flight a bold black-and-white pattern on the wings and a white rump is visible. Sexes look similar.

The range of the willet

HABITAT

Wet meadows, grassy areas of ponds and lakes, coastal salt marshes and beaches.

BEHAVIOR

Feeds by walking or wading into shallow water, and occasionally swimming in deeper water, where they pick and probe for food. Are usually in small, loose flocks or solitary. Can be very aggressive at defending territory during nesting and will fly directly at intruders to warn them off. Is one of the few species of sandpipers that will perch on posts or trees, usually the tops of evergreens.

CALLS

Is quite noisy on its breeding grounds. The most commonly heard call is a repetitive *yip-yip-yip-yip*. The willet's song is a repeated *pill-will-willet, pill-will-willet*.

FOOD

Diet includes aquatic insects, crustaceans such as crayfish and small crabs, mollusks and small fish.

A pair of willets at rest, each on one leg

FAMILY LIFE

Nests in loose colonies. Nest is a depression on open ground or hidden in vegetation. In the eastern part of North America nests are usually built on the upper part of beaches and dunes, along ponds or along the banks, ditches and streams in tidal marshes. In the west nests are on freshwater marshes. Four eggs are incubated by both parents for 22 to 29 days. The female abandons the young and mates 2 or 3 weeks after hatching. The males looks after the young for another 1 to 2 weeks before their first flight at approximately 28 days. One brood annually.

MIGRATION
Nests much farther south than most sandpipers, generally arriving on breeding grounds in April or May. Leaves on southern migration from August to September. Western breeding birds are often seen on the East Coast in fall. Year-round residents are along the southern coastal regions of the United States.

CONSERVATION CONCERNS
Species status overall in North America is secure and stable. Extensive hunting in the nineteenth and early twentieth centuries nearly caused the extinction of northeastern populations. Numbers have rebounded strongly since then and the species is now quite common. However, unlike the more northerly breeding sandpiper species that generally nest in areas remote from humans, the willet's habitat is more vulnerable to disturbance and destruction. This may be having an impact on the current population.

RELATED SPECIES
Although the willet is the only member of its genus, it is somewhat similar in appearance to the marbled godwit, and the greater and lesser yellowlegs.

A willet's breeding plumage is darker and more spotted and barred than its winter plumage

PECTORAL SANDPIPER

Calidris melanotos

A pectoral sandpiper forages on a mudflat for insects and invertebrates

This medium sized sandpiper was formerly called a grass snipe because of its preference for short or mowed grass like the snipe.

APPEARANCE
Length 9 inches. Wingspan 18 inches. Is distinguished from other sandpipers by its darker, reddish-brown head and back with fine, light striping, somewhat longer neck, a distinct line that separates the dense streaking on the breast with the whiter underbelly and greenish-yellow legs. The base of the bill is a dark, greenish yellow. The male's breast and throat appear darker.

HABITAT
Is found on grassy marshes, wet meadows, salt marshes, occasionally

tidal mudflats, muddy margins of ponds, streams, lakes and flooded fields.

The range of the pectoral sandpiper

BEHAVIOR
Usually feeds in small flocks that spread out to feed on shallow grassy marshes where the birds can be seen crouching in the grass. Often "freezes" in position at the approach of an intruder, with its neck stretched and head held high to take advantage of its cryptic coloration. Zig-zags away with a harsh cry when flushed. Feeds by moving about slowly while rapidly probing its bill into the mud. Is occasionally seen swimming. Flies in tight flocks, and sometimes associates with other sandpipers species.

CALLS
In flight makes a low, reedy *churk* sound that is hoarser than the sounds of other small shorebirds. When flushed from the ground, it makes a harsh *kreek*. During courtship the male inflates its throat immensely and gives a low hooting call.

FOOD
Insects make up the bulk of pectoral sandpipers' diet, but they also eat a variety of worms, crustaceans, spiders, algae and seeds.

FAMILY LIFE
The female builds the nest, a nicely made cup of woven grasses or leaves placed on a hummock, or other grassy area on upland tundra or a ridge. The four eggs are incubated by the female for about 22 days. The young are able to fly after approximately 21 days. Both adults depart on fall migration well before the young do. One brood per year.

MIGRATION
Generally arrives on breeding grounds in the high Arctic in May

and begins return migration to the South in July. Is often seen on migratory stopover locations until late October or early November before continuing south.

CONSERVATION CONCERNS
Species status overall in North America is secure and stable. Is quite common during migration along the East Coast and in the Midwest. Population was higher prior to being hunted extensively as a game bird in the nineteenth century.

RELATED SPECIES
The pectoral, semi-palmated, western and white-rumped sandpiper are a few of the eleven sandpipers of the genus *Calidris* that breed in North America.

When alert, the pectoral sand-piper stands tall and thin with a stretched neck

SEMI-PALMATED SANDPIPER

Calidris pusilla

A semi-palmated sandpiper sleeps with one eye open on the lookout for danger

Commonly known as "peeps" because of their plaintive call, these long-distance travelers are most commonly seen in middle latitudes during their annual migrations.

APPEARANCE
Length 6 inches. Wingspan 14 inches. Brownish gray above with white, unstreaked breasts and bellies. Their short stout bills, paler, slightly grayer upperparts and dark legs distinguish them from the similar least sandpiper. The partially webbed feet are unique among sandpipers, but are difficult observe. Sexes look alike.

HABITAT
Breeding grounds are on dry or grassy tundra, often on a ridge, usually near water. During migration (which is when we are most

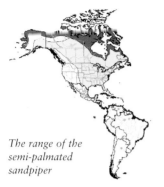

The range of the semi-palmated sandpiper

likely to see them) they are found on mudflats, coastal beaches, marshes with muddy margins, the shores of ponds and lakes and in wet meadows.

BEHAVIOR

In flight they form tight flocks. Along the mudflats of the Upper Bay of Fundy, where up to 90 percent of the entire population stops to feed before continuing southward, single flocks of over 200,000 birds have been observed. They forage by picking directly from surface or shallow probing into mud or sand.

CALLS

The commonly heard flight call is a short, shrill *cher* or *peep*. Various other chirping and peeping sounds are also heard. When frightened into flight, they utter an abrupt *ke-e-ip*.

Large congregations of semi-palmated sandpipers gather on mudflats during fall migration

FOOD
Insects, mollusks, worms and crustaceans are taken.

FAMILY LIFE
Nests on the ground in colonies. The nest, a depression on a hummock or ridge lined with grass or moss, is built by both adults. Generally four eggs are incubated by both adults for 18 to 22 days. Young are able to fly in 14 to 19 days. One brood per year.

MIGRATION
A long-distance migrant, it leaves its wintering grounds in Central and South America and flies to breeding grounds in Arctic Canada and northern Alaska every spring. After passing through the United States and southern Canada in mid-May, it arrives on its breeding grounds in early June. By late July/early August they appear in greater and greater numbers in the middle latitudes on their journey south. Hundreds of thousands stop over to feed on the Bay of Fundy mudflats to fatten up before the arduous journey south.

CONSERVATION CONCERNS
Species status overall in North America is generally secure and stable. Despite being the most abundant shorebird in North America at an estimated 3.5 million strong, the semi-palmated sandpiper's utter dependence on a few critical stopover sites during migration makes it vulnerable to catastrophic events such as oil spills.

RELATED SPECIES
There are forty-three species in the family *Scolopacidae* in North America.

Photographers Journal
I had just called it a day after the wind had come up and it started to rain. Heading home across the marsh, I noticed a semi-palmated sandpiper bracing against the driving rain on a mudflat. He paid me no mind as I sidled up beside him in the blind. As the rain grew stronger, his feathers became soaked to the skin and water splashed up from the ground, muddying his delicate breast. For

long minutes I watched in admiration as I wondered what this small bird had put behind it and what lay ahead. Where were its mates, I thought? I felt for the little bird, alone here in the rain, who knew how far from others of kind. Perhaps he was midway on a 4,500-mile journey that began on the shores of the Beaufort Sea and will end on some wetland in Colombia. Soon the squall ended and the sun began to dry the sandpiper's feathers. Before long he stretched his wings and took flight.

A semi-palmated sandpiper on a fresh-water marsh mudflat in the rain

LEAST SANDPIPER

Calidris minutilla

The smallest North American sandpiper, this least sandpiper typically forages on freshwater mudflats during migration

The least sandpiper is the smallest shorebird in North America.

APPEARANCE
Length 5–7 inches. Wingspan 13 inches. Upperparts are brown, lower parts are buff colored with a slightly streaked breast and bill is slender and black. Greenish-yellow legs distinguish this sandpiper from the very similar semi-palmated sandpiper.

HABITAT
Generally breeds in the northern parts of Canada and southern Alaska, where it nests on the tundra near ponds, and on open bogs and marshes. This is the southern-most breeding distribution of any sandpiper in the small "peep" sandpiper group, those belonging to the genus *Calidris*. Most often seen in its more southern

The range of the least sandpiper

migratory habitats such as wet meadows, mudflats, salt marshes, shores of ponds or lakes and occasionally on beaches.

BEHAVIOR

During migration it tends to scatter widely in an area among short grass or on mudflats, picking and probing for insects and invertebrates, typically doubling its weight by eating almost constantly. This is necessary to pack extra fuel into its diminutive body for the long trip ahead. When flushed, they rapidly form into a flock after take off. Mixes with other shorebird species during migration.

CALLS

The least sandpiper's vocal repertoire is fairly limited. Normally gives a soft *kweeeet* when flushed from the ground. Once in flight it gives a *greet-greet-greet* call. Males perform an in-flight courtship song on the breeding grounds.

FOOD

A variety of food such as insects, small crustaceans, worms and small mollusks is taken.

FAMILY LIFE

The nest is a depression in the moss, usually placed on a dry knoll or a hummock in a wetland. Many pairs may nest in the same area. The male does most of the incubation of the four eggs, which hatch after 19 to 23 days. The young leave the nest immediately and are able to feed themselves. Both parents tend the chicks until they are able to fly at 14 to 16 days. One brood per year.

MIGRATION

Is highly migratory and travels thousands of miles each year from its wintering grounds in the southern United States, Central

America and South America to breed in the sub-Arctic, passing northward through the United States and Canada in late April and early May. Returns south in July and August. Juveniles migrate later in fall than the adults. Will often linger on its way south and is seen well into September.

CONSERVATION CONCERNS

Species status overall in North America is secure, but the population is possibly declining. Because it is so widely distributed, it is difficult to determine population trends. Potential threats include global warming, reducing suitable breeding grounds in the North, wetland loss affecting its ability to adequately fuel up during migrations, and habitat loss on wintering grounds in Central and South America.

RELATED SPECIES

There are forty-three species in the family *Scolopacidae* in North America. Species most similar are the semi-palmated, western and white-rumped sandpipers.

The least sandpiper, like all sandpipers, is highly migratory, spending much of its life on the move

SHORT-BILLED DOWITCHER

Limnodromus griseus

A short-billed dowitcher takes a bath in the marsh

The short-billed dowitcher is one of a handful of North American shorebirds with a very long, straight bill.

APPEARANCE
Length 11 inches. Wingspan 19 inches. A medium-sized sandpiper, it is rather chunky in appearance like the common snipe with an extremely long, straight bill. The rump and lower back are bright white and conspicuous in flight. Upperparts are dark brown with lighter browns and buff on feather edges. The throat, breast and belly are a flecked reddish brown. Medium-length legs are greenish-yellow. Sexes look similar.

HABITAT
During migration (when they are most often seen) dowitchers prefer

the soft muddy margins of fresh-water and saltwater marshes, estuaries, ponds, streams and rivers, lakes, flooded fields, marine mudflats and sandy beaches. Nests in grassy tundra, wet meadows, fens and bogs.

The range of the short-billed dowitcher

BEHAVIOR

One of the most approachable, trusting shorebirds, they often feed in small flocks where they wade in the shallow water, methodically tipping their chunky bodies to front and back as they probe their long bills deep into the mud. Like many shorebird species, the tips of their bills are pliable and are able to open and close independent of the rest of the bill, at times giving the appearance of a deformity. They are adept swimmers and are often found in mixed flocks with other shorebird species during migration.

CALLS

The most commonly heard call is a soft, three-note whistle *tu-tu-tu* in a rising pitch. The flight song is a short, clear twitter.

FOOD

Diet includes aquatic insects, marine worms, mollusks, crustaceans and the seeds of aquatic plants.

FAMILY LIFE

Nest is a moss-lined depression on a hummock in open, wet, grassy tundra or muskeg. Four eggs are incubated for 21 days, mostly by the female. Young leave the nest soon after hatching. Time to first flight for young is unknown. Males have been reported rolling eggs to a new site if the nest is threatened. One brood per year.

MIGRATION

Generally arrives on its breeding grounds in April and May. Breeding begins in late May or early June. Southward migration occurs between July and late August with juveniles lingering until October to fatten up before continuing on to wintering grounds.

CONSERVATION
Species status overall in North America is secure and the population is stable. However, some suggest a possible decline. Although relatively common, the continued destruction of wintering habitats in Peru and Brazil, and the possible impact that the flooding of breeding habitats by hydroelectric dams may have had are causes for concern for the health of the short-billed dowitcher's population.

RELATED SPECIES
Its closest relative is the long-billed dowitcher, which belongs to the same genus, *Limnodromus*.

A short-billed dowditcher showing the flexibility of the tip of its long bill

WILSON'S SNIPE

Gallinago delicata

Seldom seen up close, the Wilson's snipe is nonetheless one of the most common and widespread birds in North American wetlands

An abundant member of the shorebird family, it is found in many open wetland habitats across North America.

APPEARANCE
Length 11 inches. Wingspan 19 inches. It is a stocky waterbird with an extremely long, straight bill, rear-set eyes, a whitish chin and strong horizontal striping on the head. Upperparts are mottled brown with lighter brown feather edges, the breast is a flecked brown, underparts are white and the legs are yellow-green.

HABITAT
Wet meadows, bogs, swamps, shrubby wetlands, marshes and along the edge of salt marshes. Is one of the most broadly distributed wetland birds.

BEHAVIOR

The range of the Wilson's snipe

Hunts by feel as it probes the mud with its long, pliable bill. Snipes are noted for their habit of "freezing" as a method of avoiding detection by a predator. With its effective coloration it becomes virtually invisible and doesn't attempt escape until the danger is practically upon it. At this point the snipe will burst into a violently zigzagging flight. Normal flight is steady and fast.

CALLS

It is well known for the winnowing *wooo-wooo-wooo* sound it makes as it passes overhead. This eerie sound is produced by the rush of air as it passes over vibrating tail feathers. When threatened or flushed, a loud, repetitive *weet-weet, weet-weet* call is produced.

A Wilson's snipe shows off its beautifully patterned plumage

FOOD

Will take almost any invertebrate found on the ground or in the mud, including insects (especially those in larval stages), crustaceans, mollusks and occasionally seeds.

FAMILY LIFE

Is generally a solitary nester. The female fashions a nest on the ground in a shallow scrape and lines it with grasses and other soft vegetation. Four eggs are incubated largely or exclusively by the female for 18 to 20 days. Chicks are fed by both adults and can fly after about 20 days. One brood per year.

MIGRATION
Generally arrives on breeding grounds during March and April. Southerly fall migration usually begins in October with some birds lingering until late November.

CONSERVATION CONCERNS
Species status overall in North America is secure and the population is stable. The Wilson's snipe is still quite plentiful. Population estimates put it at 2 million for North America. Despite its relative abundance, in many areas it is still hunted. We must never forget the case of the passenger pigeon, at one time the most abundant bird in North America with numbers in the billions, which became extinct in only a matter of decades due to overhunting.

RELATED SPECIES
Similar species include the American woodcock, the short-billed dowitcher and the long-billed dowitcher.

Did You Know?
Like humans, birds are visually oriented animals. They rely most heavily on the sense of sight for their survival. Some birds, such as owls and harriers, have highly binocular vision that looks forward, enabling the acute depth perception needed for hunting. Others, like woodcocks and Wilson's snipes, have less binocular vision but a wide field of view so they can watch effectively for predators practically in all directions at once. Birds that are active in the daytime, unlike most mammals, have color vision, a trait that comes in handy for many species during the selection of a mate by females where the vividness of a male's color may mean the difference in whether he mates.

RING-BILLED GULL

Larus delawarensis

The ring-billed gull forages along the edge of a lake

One of North America's most widespread and abundant gulls can be seen around near practically any body of water, fresh or salt.

APPEARANCE

Length 17 inches. Wingspan 48 inches. Adult is a medium-sized gull with a white head and underparts, a pale-gray back, relatively short, bright yellow bill with a distinctive black ring and yellow legs. Black wing tips are conspicuous during its buoyant flight. Young birds don't attain full adult plumage until the third year.

HABITAT

Freshwater lakes, ponds, marshes and rivers inland as well as coastal areas and offshore islands.

BEHAVIOR

Like most gulls, the ring-billed is a generalist forager and will take advantage of most feeding opportunities. Captures insects on the wing, feeds along coastal areas and inland shore like a shorebird where it captures crustaceans, mollusks and other invertebrates as well as fish.

The range of the ring-billed gull

Follows fishing boats for offal and in many areas frequents garbage dumps and freshly plowed agricultural fields. Frequently pirates food from species such as cormorants, terns and smaller gulls with whom it sometimes associates.

CALLS

Has typical gull cries; somewhat softer, scratchier and higher pitched than the herring gull.

FOOD

Fish, insects, worms, crustaceans, mollusks, other marine invertebrates as well as fish offal and garbage.

FAMILY LIFE

Nests in ground colonies, often with other species of gulls and terns. Both sexes participate in building the flat nest of weeds, grass and sometimes trash on an elevated spot on open ground (occasionally concealed by vegetation), usually on an island. Generally two to four eggs are incubated by both adults for 21 days. The young are tended and fed by both parents for 35 days until they leave the vicinity of the nest. One brood annually.

MIGRATION

Is migratory over most of its range, but in many places will overwinter. Spring migrants generally arrive on the breeding grounds from late March to early May and begin heading south between September and November.

CONSERVATION CONCERNS
Overall status in North America is secure and stable in the United States and Canada. Worldwide population is estimated in the millions.

RELATED SPECIES
There are over a dozen gulls belonging to *Larus*, the same genus as the ring-billed gull.

Like all gulls, ring-bills are graceful in flight

HERRING GULL

Larus argentatus

The herring gull is one of the most familiar birds in coastal areas

This highly adaptable "seagull" is the most widely distributed and abundant gull in the northern hemisphere.

APPEARANCE

Length 25 inches. Wingspan 58 inches. A large gull, by its fourth year the adult is overall white with a light slate-gray back, pinkish legs and a large yellow bill with an orange spot toward the end. Winter adults have a mottled "five o'clock shadow." Younger adults have a somewhat mottled appearance and juveniles tend to be brown.

HABITAT

Shores and islands on virtually all coasts, as well as inland on lakes, ponds, rivers, marshes, sloughs and other wetland areas.

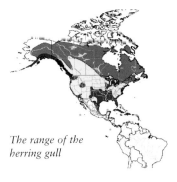

The range of the herring gull

BEHAVIOR

Is usually seen in large noisy flocks. Forages by picking food items off the ground or out of the water. Also scavenges, and in this role it cleans up the shorelines of the coast, lakes and rivers by taking stranded or dead organisms. Some feed at landfills and dumps, as well as on offal from fishing boats and fish plants. Walks and swims equally well. Is a powerful, graceful flyer that seems to relish taking wing during storms.

CALLS

Has a variety of calls, including the commonly heard *kack-kack-kack* and a *kyow-kyow-kyow* bugling sound it uses when alarmed or aroused.

FOOD

The herring gull is omnivorous and will eat just about anything it finds. This adaptability to a variety of foods no doubt contributes

A herring gull coming in for a landing

to its success as a species. Fish, crustaceans, mollusks, insects, sea urchins, young birds, eggs, amphibians and a variety of other animals are taken. Also eats seeds and berries at times when other foods are in short supply.

FAMILY LIFE
Generally nests in colonies on islands in lakes or along the coast. Male and female build a ground nest of grasses, seaweed, mosses and other materials that is lined with grass and feathers. Will occasionally nest on cliffs or in trees if suitable ground sites are unavailable. Usually three eggs are incubated by both parents for 24 to 28 days. Young leave the nest within a few hours of hatching and can fly at about 35 days, but are fed by the parents for some time after that. One brood per year.

MIGRATION
Is migratory over its northern and western breeding range. Many winter in the southern United States and along the West Coast of the continent. In eastern North America from the Great Lakes to the Atlantic Coast, it is resident year round.

CONSERVATION CONCERNS
Species status overall in North America is secure and the population is growing; extremely abundant.

RELATED SPECIES
In addition to the herring gull, there are twelve other gulls in the genus *Larus* that breed in North America.

> *Did You Know?*
> A few birds use piracy as part of the way they make a living. Kleptoparasitism, as it is known to scientists, is the act of harassing another bird in order to steal food from it. This practice isn't the exclusive domain of gulls, vultures and crows, however. Apparently mild-mannered dabbling ducks will also occasionally harass and nab food from other birds in their habitat, such as American coots.

CASPIAN TERN

Sterna caspia

A Caspian tern patrolling a lake for fish

The Caspian tern is the largest of the North American terns.

APPEARANCE

Length 21 inches. Wingspan 50 inches. Gull-like in size, this is a large tern with a pale, slate-gray back, white underparts, a black cap, heavy, red chisel-like bill and short neck and legs. Tail is not deeply forked and wings are broader than those of other terns. In flight, a darkish area on the underside of the wingtips is apparent.

HABITAT

Can be found both inland on bodies of freshwater such as marshes, lakes and ponds and in saltwater environments along beaches, and in salt marshes, lagoons and estuaries.

BEHAVIOR

Forages in the manner of other terns by plunge-diving into the water for fish. While hunting it flies with its bill pointing downward like other terns, but unlike other terns it usually hovers prior to plunging in a spectacular display of fishing prowess. Often settles on the water like a

The range of the Caspian tern

gull to feed on shrimp and other swimming crustaceans. Pirates fish from other species occasionally. Less gregarious than other terns, it is usually seen alone or in small groups, often associating with ring-billed gulls. Because of its large size, it is less buoyant in flight and more gull-like than smaller terns, and can often be seen soaring in the manner of a gull. Is a very aggressive species.

CALLS

A deep, raucous croaking of *karrrr ka-ka-ka-kow.*

FOOD

Mainly small fish, but also aquatic invertebrates.

FAMILY LIFE

Usually nests in small, but occasionally large colonies both in salt-water and freshwater wetlands. Is only rarely a solitary nester. Both sexes participate in building the nest, which is a scrape made in the sand or gravel on an island, often concealed among shells, driftwood or washed-up seaweed. Inland the nest is often placed on a heavy mat of aquatic vegetation along the shores of a lake. Nests are usually lined with moss, grass or seaweed. Generally two or three eggs are incubated by both adults for 20 to 28 days. The young can fly after 30 to 40 days but are fed by the adults for up to 8 months. One brood annually.

MIGRATION

Is migratory, except along the Gulf of Mexico and part of the southern California coast where birds are resident year round. Other birds generally arrive on their breeding grounds between March and mid-May and begin migrating south again between September and the middle of October. Most birds winter in Central America and the Caribbean.

A conservation status map of the caspian tern

CONSERVATION CONCERNS
Species status overall in North America is apparently secure and stable. Disturbance and development of nesting habitat is a major concern.

RELATED SPECIES
The caspian tern belongs to the genus *Sterna* of which there are nine other members in North America.

BLACK SKIMMER

Rynchops niger

The short legs, black-and-white coloration and long protruding lower mandible are a black skimmer's hallmarks

The black skimmer's completely unique and fascinating feeding technique sets it apart from any other species in North America.

APPEARANCE
Length 18 inches. Wingspan 44 inches. A slender bird, the size and general shape of a tern, it has very long wings relative to its body and black back, wings and back of head and neck. The front of the face, neck, breast and underparts are white. The very large, black-tipped, orange-red bill is laterally compressed (knife-like) with the lower mandible one third longer than the upper one. Has very short orange-red legs and a somewhat forked tail.

HABITAT
Coastal beaches, saltwater lagoons, salt marshes, sandbars, inlets,

The range of the black skimmer

estuaries, salt marsh creeks and occasionally rivers and fresh-water marshes.

BEHAVIOR
The defining behavior of the black skimmer is its method of foraging where, on graceful, slender wings, it carries itself just above the surface of a lagoon or other body of water with its bill open and its long lower mandible slicing through the water to capture fish. The bill can be seen snapping shut on any prey taken from the water. This is one of the most finely coordinated maneuvers in the avian world and has to be seen to be appreciated. Usually observed in small flocks, it often rests on beaches and sandbars with terns and gulls. It forages largely at night, but also early in the morning and the late evening (occasionally midday) when fish and other prey are nearer to the surface.

CALLS
Gives a low, grating, nasal *kuk-kuk-kuk* call.

FOOD
Primarily small fish, but will occasionally take surface swimming crustaceans such as shrimp.

FAMILY LIFE
Nests in colonies, occasionally with terns or gulls. Both sexes build a simple unlined scrape nest in sand or gravel, with no concealment added. Generally four eggs are incubated by both adults for 21 to 23 days. The young are fed by both adults for 23 to 25 days until they are able to fly. One brood annually.

MIGRATION
Is largely a nonmigratory permanent resident throughout most of its North American range. Birds on the mid-Atlantic coast are

migratory and usually arrive on their summer breeding grounds in April and May and head south again in September and October. There is a large permanent population in South America.

CONSERVATION CONCERNS
Overall species status in North America is secure and stable.

RELATED SPECIES
Worldwide there are three skimmer species, but only one in North America.

A black skimmer "skimming" on the wing as it hunts for small fish

DIVING BIRDS

COMMON LOON

Gavia immer

A common loon incubates on its mud nest

The loon's familiar, haunting calls have echoed through the North American wilderness for millions of years. Today, this magnificent species is an icon of the continent's wilderness.

APPEARANCE

Length 27–35 inches. Wingspan 50 inches. It is a large waterbird with a black head and neck and bold white markings on the throat and lower sides of the thick, medium-length neck. In winter, they are dark gray above and whitish below. Sexes look similar.

HABITAT

During the breeding season the common loon generally inhabits mid- to northern latitude lakes. These lakes must have a large supply of prey and be large enough for the bird to take off and

The range of the common loon

land. A suitable nesting site must also be available. In winter it frequents marine coastal areas or open freshwater.

BEHAVIOR

The best known behavior is the call that the male, especially, uses when establishing and defending breeding territories and communicating with its mate and young. Visual displays during courtship and territorial posturing are also performed. The loon is an efficient fisher that swims underwater with powerful legs and large webbed feet. Prey are swallowed underwater. Does not come out of the water, except when nesting. Requires a long, laborious run across the surface to get airborne. Flight is powerful and direct.

CALLS

"He uttered a long-drawn unearthly howl, probably more like a wolf than any other bird." Here Henry David Thoreau was probably referring to the "wail-call" given by both males and females to help locate one another. Lasting about two seconds, it contains a distinct rise in pitch, sometimes ending on a lower note. The "tremelo-call," a short tremulous note lasting about half a second, is given by both sexes at the appearance of an intruder or a disturbance. The "yodel-call" is a complex undulating call uttered by only the male and usually signals territorial ownership.

FOOD

Mainly fish, but also amphibians, crabs, crayfish, shellfish and aquatic insects.

FAMILY LIFE

The nest is a mass of aquatic vegetation built at the edge of the water, usually on a small island for protection from predators. Male and female take part in the nest building. The two eggs are incubated in turn by both adults for 26 to 31 days. Chicks leave the nest one day after the last egg has hatched. They will frequently ride on the adults' backs for up to 3 weeks after hatching. After 75 to 80 days the young make their first flight. Will occasionally try a second laying if the first attempt failed.

MIGRATION
Arrives on northerly breeding lakes soon after ice breakup in March to June (in more northerly areas). Fall migration occurs from September to December, with most birds overwintering in marine coastal areas and inland lakes in the vicinity of 35 degrees latitude and south. First-year young do not migrate south, but shift to the east or west to marine coastal areas.

CONSERVATION CONCERNS
Species status overall in North America is apparently secure, but may be declining in the U.S. In Canada (where about 90 percent of the continent's common loons breed) the population is considered secure and stable. Acid rain, industrial pollution (especially mercury), the ingestion of lead shot from the

A conservation status map of the common loon

bottom of lakes, loss of nesting habitat along lake shores and disturbance caused by boats all affect the loon's breeding success.

RELATED SPECIES
There are four other species of loons in North America.

Photographer's Journal
After relieving its mate on the nest, a common loon gently turns its eggs to ensure they are evenly incubated. Nesting loons are extremely wary of intruders and are one of the most difficult birds to photograph at close range. I had to plan my approach carefully to avoid disturbing them. I entered the blind out of view so they wouldn't associate me with it. To allow the birds to get comfortable in the presence of the blind, I spent some time each day for

about a week moving across the pond, in full view, at the edge of their nesting territory. Finally, it was time to get close enough to photograph the birds. One cold May morning at about 4:30 a.m., I began inching my way across the little cove toward the nest.

After a couple of hours I was in position with a telephoto lens. The loons showed no interest in the blind. While I was waiting for better light, the nesting bird let out a soft hoot call, signalling its mate to come and take its place on the nest. I was lucky enough to photograph the newly arrived bird arranging the eggs before it began a long stint of incubation.

A common loon turns the eggs on its nest to ensure they are properly incubated

Did You Know?

One of the oldest, most unchanged families of birds is the loons, which have been around in one form or another for tens of millions of years. The idea that birds are evolved from small dinosaurs goes back to the discovery of the *Archaeopteryx lithographica* fossil in the mid-1800s. This small fossil, found in a quarry in Germany, preserved the earliest known specimen of a bird-like animal. Complete with wings and fine impressions of feathers, the fossil nevertheless looked very much like a small theropod dinosaur. Were it not for the feathers, it would have undoubtedly been classified as a dinosaur.

PIED-BILLED GREBE

Podilymbus podiceps

Pied-billed grebes will frequently carry their young during the first few weeks of life

Despite being a shy, seldom-seen bird, the pied-billed grebe is practically ubiquitous in North American marshes.

APPEARANCE
Length 13 inches. Wingspan 20 inches. On the water it looks somewhat like a tiny duck: brown with a black bib on the chin and upper throat, a black ring around the short, chicken-like bill and a white ring around the eye.

HABITAT
It prefers heavily vegetated freshwater marshes, and is often seen in open water, but also haunts the edges of cattail swales and other aquatic vegetation. They require a small amount of open water for taking off. In winter it will often inhabit brackish estuaries.

The range of the pied-billed grebe

BEHAVIOR

Moves slowly while on the surface. Dives for food, usually staying submerged for less than 15 seconds. Will often surface some distance from where it first submerged. When it senses danger, it will slowly submerge its body first, leaving just its head sticking out of the water before completely disappearing. May surface some distance away, sometimes under the cover of dense vegetation. Will also splash-dive into the water as it flees danger. Males can be very aggressive during defense of its territory, often attacking its own species and others from underwater. Takes flight infrequently during the breeding season.

CALLS

Is quite vocal during breeding season. The most commonly heard call is a loud *kuk-kuk-kow-kow-kow-kow-cowp-cowp*, the syllables growing longer and more slurred toward the end. Other sounds include a single soft *koo* used infrequently when alarmed.

FOOD

Almost anything small enough to swallow, including small fish, aquatic insects, frogs, leeches and snails.

A pied-billed grebe rears up out of the marsh and stretches its short wings

FAMILY LIFE

The nest is a bulky mass of floating, decaying plant matter about 12 inches in diameter, anchored in shallow water, usually under the cover of cattails or other heavy vegetation. Adults will sometimes approach the nest underwater to conceal its location. Four to eight eggs are usually laid and are incubated for about 23 days, largely by the female. The newly hatched young can swim and dive immediately.

Tiny, young chicks will often hitch rides on their parents' back, often up to three or four at a time. The adults dive for food and present it to the chicks upon surfacing. Young will generally stay in the same part of the marsh until the fall migration. One or two broods per year.

MIGRATION

Generally arrives on northerly breeding grounds soon after the ice breaks up in April or May. Fall migration occurs during September to November. Is year-round resident over much of the southern United States.

CONSERVATION CONCERNS

Species status overall in North America is secure, but the population appears to be declining. Some surveys have shown an average of a 2 percent per year population decline between 1966 and 1993.

RELATED SPECIES

There are six other species of grebe in North America.

Did You Know?
Some wetland birds carry their young. Not only is it quite common to see a baby pied-billed grebe (or several) or a common loon hitching a ride on mom's or dad's back, but there is anecdotal evidence that some species will even carry their young in flight! Carrying is done to transport the young across stretches of water where they might be vulnerable to predators. But anyone who's watched a pied-billed grebe family would swear the young ones simply crawl up on the adult's back because they just don't feel like swimming!

DIVING BIRDS

AMERICAN WHITE PELICAN

Pelecanus erythrorhynchos

The white pelican, although a graceful flier, is the heaviest of all wetland birds, weighing 17 pounds

This magnificent species is the largest and one of the heaviest (second only to the trumpeter swan) native wetland birds in North America.

APPEARANCE
Length 62 inches. Wingspan 108 inches. It is an unmistakably large white bird with an enormous orange-yellow bill and pouch and short, orange-yellow legs. In flight the trailing part of wing and wing tip are conspicuously black. Holds its neck in a slight "S" with head drawn back while resting the heavy bill on the breast. Flies by alternately flapping and gliding.

HABITAT
Inland lakes and coastal areas such as estuaries and lagoons that

are suitably shallow for its specialized foraging techniques. Breeds on islands in freshwater lakes.

The range of the American white pelican

BEHAVIOR

Generally feeds alone or in small groups by scooping fish out of the water. Will also occasionally forage cooperatively. Once a school of fish is located, a group of white pelicans will gather in a line offshore somewhat and herd the fish toward shore by beating the water with their wings. Once the fish are in shallow enough water, the birds scoop them up, drain off the excess water from their pouches, then swallow them. Does not dive like the brown pelican.

CALLS

Silent, except in breeding colony where it gives guttural croaks and grunts.

FOOD

Almost entirely fish, but will also eat crustaceans.

DIVING BIRDS

These white pelicans are feeding communally by driving a school of fish into shallowed water where they can be scooped up

FAMILY LIFE

Nests exclusively in dense colonies on flat ground. Both sexes build a scrape in the earth with surrounding dirt, plant stems, bits of wood and other fine material that is drawn up to create a rim around the eggs. Generally two eggs are incubated by both sexes for 29 to 36 days. Both parents feed the young until their first flight at 60 days or more. One brood annually.

MIGRATION

Entire population is migratory. Birds migrate to inland breeding areas in the north-central interior of the continent in spring and move to wintering areas (mostly coastal, but also inland lakes) in southern parts of the continent and southward to Central America.

CONSERVATION CONCERNS

Overall species status in North America is vulnerable in the United States, apparently secure and stable in Canada where the majority of the species's seventy or so breeding colonies are located. Although the population may be increasing overall, most of its breeding colonies are highly threatened by habitat loss and fluctuating water levels due to drought and dams. Low water levels improve access for mammals that prey on the eggs, reducing the pelican's reproductive success. Shooting of white pelicans is a major cause of mortality.

A conservation status map of the American white pelican

RELATED SPECIES

The other North American pelican species is the brown pelican.

BROWN PELICAN

Pelecanus occidentalis

A group of brown pelicans drifting between waves

This striking bird, the world's smallest species of pelican, is exceptionally beautiful in flight as it skims so close to the surface of the water that it practically touches it with its wing tips.

APPEARANCE

Length 51 inches. Wingspan 79 inches. This is a large bird with a streaked silvery-brown back, extremely large whitish head with a yellow forecrown, an enormous bill, similar in shape to the white pelican's, white and dark brown striped neck, blackish brown breast and underparts and short gray legs. At a distance it appears much darker overall than the white pelican. In flight the neck is an S-shape with the head drawn in to support the head and bill on the breast. Flies by alternately flapping and gliding.

HABITAT

Various open coastal habitats. Rarely seen inland, except in California's Salton Sea where it is common. Feeds on open coastlines, but rests in estuaries, lagoons and other shallow water areas.

The range of the brown pelican

BEHAVIOR

Has a spectacular foraging technique. On spotting a fish while patrolling over the water at an altitude of 30 feet or so, the brown pelican will turn sharply and head into a vertical dive with its bill thrust forward and its wings half folded behind it. It impacts the water with a great splash and is carried beneath its surface with its bill open wide, scooping up fish near the surface. Terns sometimes take fish from the pelican. They are gregarious and usually fly in small groups, sometimes large, in single file, gliding for long distances on the momentum gained from updrafts created by the waves.

CALLS

Is largely silent except for some low clucking. Young are more vocal.

The brown pelican often rests in wetlands such as lagoons and salt marshes

FOOD
Mostly fish, but also free-swimming crustaceans such as shrimp.

FAMILY LIFE
Is a colonial nester, usually on small islands. Both sexes participate in building a nest of sticks, twigs, reeds and grasses on the ground or in the tops of low brushy trees such as mangroves. Tree nests tend to be more elaborate than ground nests, which might be little more than a scrape in the earth. Generally, three eggs are incubated by both adults for 28 to 30 days. Young are fed by both parents for 71 to 88 days until they can fly. One brood annually.

MIGRATION
Birds breeding in more northerly parts of the range along the Atlantic and Pacific coasts winter along the southern coasts of North America, as well as Central and South America.

CONSERVATION CONCERNS
Overall status in North America is apparently secure and stable, but is still listed as an endangered or threatened species in parts of the United States. Population crashed in the mid-1900s due to eggshell thinning brought on by widespread pesticide use. Population is recovering.

RELATED SPECIES
The other pelican in North America is the American white pelican.

A conservation status map of the brown pelican

ANHINGA

Anhinga anhinga

Anhingas are also known as snake-birds because of their long, sinuous necks

This distant relative of the cormorant is one of the most unusual North American wetland birds. It is also known as the snake-bird for its habit of swimming with only its serpentine neck and small head protruding from the water.

APPEARANCE
Length 35 inches. Wingspan 45 inches. Practically everything about this bird seems long. It is a slender, overall black waterbird with a long, kinked neck, and has a small head with a bright red eye and pointed, dull yellow bill, long fan-shaped tail and slender, pointed wings. Female's neck and head are brown, male's are black. In flight the long fanned tail and whitish patch on the underside of the wings are apparent. It is a strong flyer with a quick wing beat.

HABITAT

Freshwater swamps, lakes, deeper sections of freshwater marshes, man-made canals, sluggish streams. Prefers wetlands with suitable roosting trees nearby.

The range of the anhinga

BEHAVIOR

Forages by swimming underwater and spearing fish with its bill. Upon surfacing will toss the fish into the air, catch it in its bill, then begin swallowing it head first. Excellent at controlling its buoyancy like a grebe, allowing it to sink without having to surface dive. Avoids fishing in salt water. Often soars like a hawk, sometimes to great heights. Is quite awkward when moving about in trees. (I even saw one fall completely out of a tree once. Luckily it landed in the water!)

CALLS

Has hoarse, guttural croaking call in the manner of a cormorant. Also makes a quick clicking noise, *kuk-kuk-kuk*.

FOOD

Mainly fish, but also crustaceans, frogs, water snakes and other invertebrates.

FAMILY LIFE

Is generally a colonial nester, often in association with herons and egrets. Both sexes participate in building the nest, a bulky platform of sticks, twigs, leaves, etc., lined with softer plant material such as leaves and stems. Nest is placed in a low tree. Occasionally appropriates the nests of smaller herons and egrets. Generally four eggs are incubated for 26 to 29 days by both adults. Young are fed regurgitated food by both parents before finally leaving the nest.

MIGRATION
Is generally nonmigratory, although some individuals winter in Mexico.

CONSERVATION CONCERNS
Species status in North America is secure and stable.

RELATED SPECIES
Is the only anhinga in North America, a member of the worldwide *Darter* family.

Did You Know?
The single feature that distinguishes birds from all other animals is feathers. Other animals have wings and can fly, lay eggs, have beaks, sing or build nests, but no other animal has feathers, as all birds do. Birds produce feathers in large numbers, from about 1,000 in a hummingbird to 25,000 or so in swans and must continue to do so throughout their lives to replace those that are worn or damaged. They are not only used in flight, but for temperature regulation and in adorning males with breeding colors.

Anhinga drying it wings

DOUBLE-CRESTED CORMORANT

Phalacrocorax auritus

Double-crested cormorants float low in the water

This familiar waterbird is the most common species of cormorant in North America.

APPEARANCE
Length 32 inches. Wingspan 52 inches. It is a large, all black or dark brown bird, roughly similar in shape to a loon. The long, hooked bill is bright yellow. Cormorants float very low in the water with the top of the back and the head and neck visible. The tail is completely submerged. The small white head crests, for which the species is named, are seldom seen but more visible in western birds.

HABITAT
At home in both freshwater and salt water, it is found in almost any open water such as lakes, swamps, marshes, rivers and marine

The range of the double-crested cormorant

coastal areas as long as there is suitable food available, the water is deep enough and they have enough room to take off.

BEHAVIOR

An efficient underwater hunter, its dives often last 30 seconds or longer. Brings fish to surface before eating. The double-crested cormorant is a very strong flyer. Over larger bodies of water, groups are often seen in low flight in a V-formation. Getting into the air is a different story, with a lot of running and splashing before takeoff. Regularly perches with its wings spread to dry the

Double-crested cormorants are powerful flyers

feathers, particularly a layer of waterproof, insulating feathers against the skin.

CALLS
Is largely silent except near the nest where a variety of guttural croaking sounds are made during courtship.

FOOD
Fish are eaten almost exclusively. Various sizes and species are taken. Will occasionally take aquatic invertebrates.

FAMILY LIFE
Nests in colonies ranging from a few individuals to hundreds of birds, often mixing with nesting herons and egrets. Both male and female participate in building the nest, which is placed either on the ground or in a tree. Both birds incubate the three or four eggs for about 28 days. Newly hatched young are fed regurgitated food by both parents for the next 40 days or so until they can fly on their own and leave the nest area. One brood per year.

MIGRATION
Birds usually begin to arrive on the breeding grounds in March, with the peak migration during April and May. By October most of them will have left on the migration south. Many birds along the coasts are year-round residents.

CONSERVATION CONCERNS
Species status overall in North America is secure and population is possibly increasing. Despite having been decimated by DDT in the mid-twentieth century, the population of the double-crested cormorant is generally increasing across North America. However, many other cormorant species around the world are vulnerable to extinction.

RELATED SPECIES
There are six members of the cormorant family in North America.

We often see birds such as double-crested cormorants, ducks or shorebirds flying low over the water, practically skimming the surface and sometimes even following the contours of the waves. They do this for a good reason. Flying very close to the water allows the birds to take advantage of the "ground effect." This aerodynamic principal reduces drag as the shape of the air currents flowing beneath the wings are altered by their interaction with the water's surface. This reduces the energy a bird must expend in flight. Because the effect works only when the wing is extremely close to the surface, birds rarely take advantage of it over land where the chance of colliding with an obstacle is much greater.

PERCHING BIRDS

BELTED KINGFISHER

Ceryle alcyon

Kingfishers often use whatever convenient perch gives them a commanding view of the water below

No North American wetland would seem complete without the raucous belted kingfisher and its abrasive rattling call.

APPEARANCE

Length 13 inches. Wingspan 20 inches. It is somewhat songbird-like in appearance, with a head that looks entirely too large for its body. The head is topped by a crest, with a white spot in front of the eye and a long, heavy, black bill. Bluish-gray upperparts extend in a wide band across the upper breast. The more colorful female adds a reddish-brown band across the belly and on the flanks. Both have white underparts and tiny legs and feet. Its flight technique is a distinctive intermittent flapping interspersed with short, almost imperceptible glides.

HABITAT

Virtually any wetland where the water is deep enough for it to dive, such as lakes, ponds, swamps, wooded streams, marshes, salt marshes, salt creeks, lagoons and estuaries.

The range of the belted kingfisher

BEHAVIOR

Is solitary and forages by diving headfirst into the water in spectacular fashion, either from a perch or from flight. Often hovers for a while as it searches for fish before diving. Is extremely skittish and generally flees while giving its rattling call at the merest sight of a human, making it very difficult to approach. Frequents favorite perches such as snags and branches hanging over the water.

CALLS

A lengthy, loud and varying rattle, *ke-ke-ke-ke-ke-ke-ke.*

A female belted kingfisher watches and waits on its hunting perch

FOOD
Mainly fish, but also takes aquatic invertebrates, frogs, salamanders, lizards, insects and occasionally mice. Will rarely eat berries.

FAMILY LIFE
Both sexes participate in excavating a horizontal or slightly upslanted burrow in a vertical embankment, usually near water. Burrow is usually 3–6 feet in length, occasionally up to 16 feet in length. Nesting chamber at the end of the tunnel is normally bare, but is sometimes lined by leaves. Generally six or seven eggs are incubated by both adults for 23 or 24 days. Young are fed by both parents for 27 to 29 days until they leave the nest.

MIGRATION
Is migratory through the northern half of its range, and a year-round resident in the southern half. Migratory birds generally arrive on breeding grounds in March or April and generally leave on their southerly migration in early fall.

CONSERVATION CONCERNS
Species status overall in North America is secure and stable. Has one of the largest ranges of any North American bird.

RELATED SPECIES
The ringed kingfisher and the green kingfisher both have very limited ranges within North America.

PERCHING BIRDS

ALDER FLYCATCHER

Empidonax alnorum

An alder flycatcher perched and watching for insects to capture on the wing

A sharp eye is needed to see this dull-colored little flycatcher as it sallies forth from its perch in a wooded wetland to pluck insects from midair.

APPEARANCE

Length 6 inches. Wingspan 9 inches. It is a small, sparrow-sized bird with an overall dull olive-green back and a lighter belly. The dark gray wings show two distinctly white horizontal bars. The tail is quite long and the head appears large with a white ring around the eye and a long, broad bill that is black on the top and pale orange underneath. The throat and chin are white. Sexes look alike. Most flycatchers in the *Empidonax* genus are very similar and difficult to tell apart.

HABITAT

Generally inhabits alder and willow thickets around swamps, wet meadows, streams, freshwater marshes, fens and bogs.

The range of the alder flycatcher

BEHAVIOR

Although shy and difficult to see, the alder flycatcher is an extremely active bird that forages by sallying forth from a favorite perch to capture insects in midair before immediately returning to its perch. Hunts mostly in the alder thickets and low brush surrounding a wet meadow or swamp. Flycatchers in general have somewhat long wings for their size, giving them incredible agility and quickness in the air.

CALLS

Is virtually silent except during breeding season. The male alder flycatcher's song is a wheezing *ree-bee-o*. Its song is the only way to positively distinguish it from the very closely related willow flycatcher whose song is a slurred *fitz-bew*. The two species are so similar that until quite recently they were considered the same species, called a Traill's flycatcher. Calls of the alder flycatcher include a simple *pit* and *zee-oo*.

FOOD

Diet is primarily flying insects, but also includes other crawling insects, spiders and other invertebrates. Berries and seeds are also sometimes consumed.

FAMILY LIFE

The untidy, cup-shaped nest is placed in the crotch of a bush or small tree. It is made of grass, plant stems, bark and other fibers and lined with fine grasses, plant down and pine needles. The female generally incubates three or four eggs for 12 to 14 days. The young are tended by both parents and make their first flight after about 13 days. One brood per year.

MIGRATION

A neotropical migrant that winters in north-central South America, it generally arrives on its breeding grounds in May or June. Departs on its southerly migration during August and September.

CONSERVATION CONCERNS

Species status overall in North America is secure and the population is stable or increasing. Is relatively common within its range.

RELATED SPECIES

Including the alder flycatcher, there are ten species of flycatchers in the genus *Empidonax*. The most similar in appearance and behavior is the willow flycatcher.

TREE SWALLOW
Tachycineta bicolor

A tree swallow feeds its young damselflies and other flying insects it captures over the marsh

The tree swallow is one of the most anticipated birds of spring. Nothing can match the grace of a tree swallow hunting dragonflies and other insects over a summer marsh.

APPEARANCE
Length 5 inches. Wingspan 14 inches. Is superbly adapted for flight and is streamlined with relatively long wings. White below, fully mature adults are an iridescent blue-green above. The female is dark brown above until getting its full adult plumage in its second year. Has very short legs and small feet and is broad headed with a wide, gaping bill to catch insects. Tail is slightly forked.

HABITAT
Is found in most open environments with high insect populations

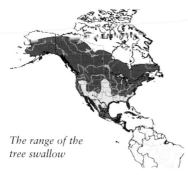

The range of the tree swallow

such as freshwater marshes, wet meadows, fens and bogs.

BEHAVIOR

The hallmark behavior of the tree swallow is its amazing flight. Hunts on the wing by snatching insects from the air with its wide mouth. Often hunts in groups over the marsh in a zigzagging cloud of wings when food is plentiful. Roosts communally at night, and where suitable nesting sites are available, they will breed in loose colonies. Associates closely with other swallow species.

CALLS

Although tree swallows are classified as songbirds, they have a very limited repertoire of sounds. Most commonly heard is a liquidy,

A tree swallow in flight with nutritious insects for its hungry young

gurgling sound usually uttered by birds in flight. Alarm call is a forceful and rapidly repeated *chee-tut chee-tut*. The male's courtship song is a series of three long descending notes capped off with a warble.

FOOD
Insects caught in the air, but also those gleaned from trees, shrubs and from the ground. It is the only swallow species that can eat seeds and berries (such as waxy bayberries) over an extended period of time. This may be one reason they can overwinter as far north as coastal Long Island, New York.

FAMILY LIFE
Preferred nesting site is in a cavity in a dead tree, usually 3–13 feet above the ground, located near water. Artificial nesting boxes are also used. Most of the nest cavity preparation is done by the female. She builds a cup of dry grass and lines it with feathers to create a soft bed for the four to six eggs she will lay. Incubation lasts 13 to 16 days and is done by the female alone. When she leaves the nest to feed, the male will guard the eggs, but doesn't incubate. Young are fed by both adults. After about 30 days the young can fly and leave the nest for good. One and occasionally two broods.

MIGRATION
Generally arrives on breeding grounds in late March to early May. Fall migration occurs soon after breeding in late July, peaking in late September to October.

CONSERVATION CONCERNS
Species status overall in North America is secure and population is stable. The increased use of nest boxes has helped maintain a healthy population of tree swallows.

RELATED SPECIES
There are seven other species of swallows in North America, including the purple martin.

Tree swallows are some of the most masterful flyers of the avian world. They swoop and dive gracefully through the air the way an otter swims through the sea. Capturing images of them doing this is anything but graceful. There are no tricks; just patience, familiarity, good timing, and a little luck. This particular bird was zooming about its nest, which was located in a hole in a broken tree at the edge of a fen. Tree swallows can be approached near the nest so long as one doesn't get close enough to disturb them. I stood a few feet behind the nesting tree and observed the bird flying in and out as it brought payload after payload of juicy dragonflies for the little family ensconced inside. Once I had a good idea of its flight path, I pre-focused my lens and simply waited for it to arrive. I was able to capture it just right in the warm evening light of early summer. Unfortunately, "the universal wildlife photographer's rule" came into play at about that time— the beauty of the light increases in direct proportion to the number of hungry mosquitoes!

An aerial hunter par excellence, this tree swallow has a little cargo of succulent flying insects

YELLOW WARBLER

Dendroica petechia

The yellow warbler is one of the tiniest, yet most brilliantly colored of all birds found in wetlands

This bright yellow bird is unmistakable as it flits from place to place among the moist thickets and bushes that surround a wetland.

APPEARANCE
Length 5 inches. Wingspan 8 inches. An all-yellow warbler, it is slightly olive-yellow on top. The dark eyes contrast dramatically with the bright yellow face. Male has red or orange vertical streaks on its breast; the female is similar except it lacks streaks. Has a slender black bill. The inner webs of the tail show large yellow patches that distinguish it from other warblers

HABITAT
Prefers moist areas with dense thickets of alders, willows, briers and other vegetation along the edges of marshes, bogs, fens,

The range of the yellow warbler

streams or lakes. Also likes garden shrubbery.

BEHAVIOR
Is quite noticeable as it forages on the stems and leaves of trees, bushes and briers, etc. It deftly makes its way among the foliage nabbing small caterpillars. Yellow warblers will often "hawk" insects by flying from a perch to snap them in mid-air. The male tends to feed in higher, less dense vegetation than the female, perhaps to be more visible to other males that may enter its territory.

CALLS
Is somewhat geographically variable song is a lovely, bright, somewhat slurred phrase *tsee-tsee-tsee-tsee-sitta-wee-tsee* that carries well across the open country of the wetland. Call is a simple *chip*.

FOOD
Diet consists mainly of insects, larvae and berries.

FAMILY LIFE
Built largely by the female, the nest is a cup placed in the fork of a tree or bush, normally 3–13 feet high (sometimes higher). Materials used include grasses, weed stems, moss, lichen and spider's silk and nest is lined with animal hair, downy plant matter and fine grasses. Three to six eggs are incubated by the female for about 12 days. The young birds are tended by both parents before their first flight at 9 to 12 days. One to two broods per year.

MIGRATION
Normally arrives on its breeding grounds in April or May (earlier in more southerly areas of its range). Fall migration generally occurs from late July to early September.

CONSERVATION CONCERNS
Species status overall in North America is secure with possible population decline in parts of its range. Loss of river and streamside habitat may be responsible. This extremely-wide ranging bird is quite plentiful in its preferred habitat across North America.

RELATED SPECIES
Is part of the wood-warbler family with fifty-three species in North America. Its genus, *Dendroica*, includes twenty other species, including the prairie, Cape May and magnolia warblers, which all show considerable yellow.

Yellow warblers frequent the alders that grow in wetlands

COMMON YELLOWTHROAT

Geothlypis trichas

Common yellowthroats, like this female, are one of the most common song-birds around many wetlands

One of the most commonly seen small songbirds of the wetlands, this highly animated and colorful member of the warbler family is a perennial favorite of nature enthusiasts.

APPEARANCE
Length 5 inches. Wingspan 7 inches. A small warbler, the male is a pale olive green on the upperparts and lower belly area with a bright yellow throat and a distinctive black mask. Tail is rounded and the bill is black and thin. The female is similar, but lacks the black mask and is a little duller.

HABITAT
Cattails and rushes in freshwater and saltwater marshes, thickets

along the edges of wet meadows and bogs, bushes and shrubs around clearings. Prefers moist areas, but is found in drier places as well.

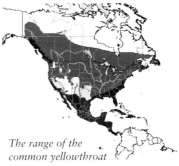

The range of the common yellowthroat

BEHAVIOR
Is very energetic and feeds quite close to the ground, often concealed deep in the midst of vegetation. Flits from plant to plant, climbing vertically up and down stems or is on the ground gleaning insects from leaves and grass. Flights tend to be short and jerky and usually just a few feet from one clump of vegetation to the next. The female is less often observed. Occasionally catches insects in midair.

CALLS
The male's song, sung from a low perch, is a bright and rollicking *witchery-witchery-witchery-witch*, reminiscent of a squeaky wheel spinning. The song varies geographically. Also has a husky *tsip*, which it may repeat several times.

FOOD
A varied assortment of insects, larvae, spiders and seeds is taken.

FAMILY LIFE
A bulky nest of dead leaves and grasses is usually built by the female on the ground under a tangle of briers or other vegetation. The three to five eggs are incubated by the female for 12 days. Both parents tend the young until they become fledglings after about 10 days. Two broods per year.

MIGRATION
Generally arrives on its breeding grounds in early April to late May (earlier in the south). Fall migration occurs from late August to late October.

CONSERVATION CONCERNS

Species status overall in North America is secure and stable, although one survey has shown significant declines in parts of its North American range. Is possibly the most abundant warbler in North America.

RELATED SPECIES

A member of the warbler family, the common yellowthroat is the only species in its genus, but has up to fourteen subspecies across North America.

A male common yellowthroat in breeding plumage

SAVANNAH SPARROW

Passerculus sandwichensis

The yellow accents on the front of the head (an area called the lores) of the savannah sparrow are apparent here

Of all the sparrows, none is more at home in the open grassy areas that border marshes and other wetlands.

APPEARANCE
Length 5 inches. Wingspan 7 inches. Is a smaller sparrow with a short, notched tail, fine streaking on the breast, white belly and flesh-colored legs. The bill is relatively small, pointed and pinkish. The lores (the area just above the base of the bill in front of the eyes) tend to be yellow. A whitish stripe runs from front to back on the middle of the crown and the throat is buff-colored or white. Sexes look alike.

HABITAT
Inhabits a wide variety of open habitats such as fresh and salt

The range of the savannah sparrow

marshes, wet meadows, bogs, fens, grassy dunes and grasslands.

BEHAVIOR

Spends most of its time on the ground where it forages in the grass, occasionally scratching in the soil to find food. When approached, it will often run away through the grass instead of taking flight. Is usually seen perching on low vegetation and fence posts. In flight it carries itself low to the ground on short, rapidly beating wings, rarely flying more than a few feet high.

CALLS

Has an unusual song that sounds like little more than a prolonged wheezing or buzzing, almost a whisper-like *tik-tik-tseee-tsuuuuuu*. Its basic call note is a simple and weak *tseek*.

Savannah sparrows are common in the open areas surrounding wetlands

FOOD
Diet includes seeds, as well as insects, snails, spiders and other small invertebrates.

FAMILY LIFE
The female builds a nest of grass and plant stems in a hollow scrape in the ground that is lined by fine materials and sheltered by grasses or other vegetation. Three to five eggs are incubated for 10 to 13 days by both parents. Young are tended by both adults until they can fly at 7 to 14 days. One to two broods per year.

MIGRATION
Generally arrives on its breeding grounds in March through May. Fall migration occurs from September to November.

CONSERVATION CONCERNS
Species status overall in North America is secure and stable. Although abundant and widespread across the continent, two subspecies of the savannah sparrow are endangered. On the East Coast, *Passerculus sandwichensis princeps*, formerly thought to be a separate species called the Ispwich sparrow, nests only on Sable Island in the Atlantic Ocean off Nova Scotia. Only a few thousand pairs of this federally endangered bird remain. On the West Coast, in Santa Barbara County, California, the Belding's savannah sparrow's population totals only a few thousand birds, placing it on the state's endangered species list.

RELATED SPECIES
Although the savannah sparrow is the only bird in the genus *Passerculus*, it is similar, both in habit and appearance, to the song sparrow.

SONG SPARROW

Melospiza melodia

Song sparrows are aptly named, singing complex and beautiful songs

This drab and inconspicuous little sparrow brings a measure of warmth to the early days of spring with its melodious song. It is one of the most widespread birds in North America, with over thirty subspecies.

APPEARANCE
Length 6 inches. Wingspan 8 inches. A stocky bird with a relatively long tail, it has a short semi-conical bill. It is heavily streaked in brown, especially on the underparts, and has brown and gray stripes on the crown and one broad stripe down each side of the front of the throat that enclose a small white patch. Streaks on the breast converge to form a large dark spot in the middle and it has dull, pinkish, flesh-toned legs. Sexes look alike.

HABITAT

Is widespread across a number of habitat types. In wetlands, it frequents the bushy margins of marshes, lakes, wet meadows, alder thickets and other bodies of water. Is also found in upland areas near salt marshes.

The range of the song sparrow

BEHAVIOR

Is generally seen in low brush and shrubs as it gleans insects. Flies low on rapidly beating wings no more than 6–10 feet from the ground. Males are highly territorial during the breeding season and often engage in chases. Forages in low trees, bushes, grass and on the ground. Is often seen scratching the ground to get at seeds.

CALLS

The hallmark of the song sparrow is its beautiful territorial singing. Is heard primarily during spring, but also later in the summer for a time. This spectacular song, which is sung from a series of perches around its territory, is complex and varied. It usually begins with two or three clear whistled notes, followed by a varied trill. Also has a simple, single *tsimp* and *tseet*.

FOOD

Insects, spiders, larvae, seeds, berries, tiny crustaceans and mollusks in coastal areas.

FAMILY LIFE

Constructed by the female, the nest is a small, cup-shaped affair of grass, leaves and strips of bark lined with soft materials such as very fine grass and cattail down. It is built on the ground, beneath a low bush, brush pile or shrub. The female incubates the three or four eggs for 12 to 14 days. Both parents tend the young for 9 to 16 days until they make their first flight. Two or three broods each year.

MIGRATION
Most of the birds in the northern third of the range are migratory. Generally arrives on breeding grounds in March or April and leaves by late October in most places. Individuals often overwinter, even in the northern part of its range, in part relying on bird feeders.

CONSERVATION CONCERNS
Species status overall in North America is secure and stable. The subspecies *graminea* of Santa Barbara Island, California, became extinct after introduced rabbits destroyed its habitat.

RELATED SPECIES
There are about thirty subspecies of song sparrows in North America. Two separate species, the swamp sparrow and Lincoln's sparrow, both belong to the same genus *Melospiza*.

A wind-blown song sparrow

SWAMP SPARROW

Melospiza georgiana

Swamp sparrows forage by scrambling among the undergrowth of emergent plants such as cattails

You are likely to detect this aptly named little sparrow first by its sweet trilling song almost anywhere there is fresh water and enough emergent vegetation for it to make its home.

APPEARANCE
Length 6 inches. Wingspan 7 inches. It is a typical sparrow, similar in appearance to the song sparrow but slightly smaller. Overall it appears rufous above with black streaking, and has a gray unstreaked breast, buff underparts, a chestnut crown and a gray bill.

HABITAT
Emergent vegetation around freshwater marshes, bogs, sluggish streams and wet meadows or wet areas with shrubbery such as

The range of the swamp sparrow

willow and alders. Favors tangled vegetation.

BEHAVIOR
Spends most of its time skulking, often wading on waterlogged vegetation among the cattails, reeds and rushes where it gleans it food. Males are typically seen singing to establish a territory while perched atop cattails and rushes.

CALLS
Song is a simple, loud and slow musical trill *tweeta-tweeta-tweeta* repeated many times and fading at the end. Other calls are a simple one-syllable *chip* and a *zeet*.

FOOD
Diet includes grass, sedge and forb seeds as well as insects.

FAMILY LIFE
The cup-shaped nest is built by the female in a low bush or on a tussock of marsh vegetation, sedge or grass, often directly over water and lined with fine grass. Four or five eggs are incubated by the female for 12 to 15 days. Both parents tend the young for 11 to 13 days until the young can fly. Two broods per year.

MIGRATION
Spring migrants generally arrive on the breeding grounds in mid-April to mid-May. Fall migration generally occurs from late September to mid-October. Most birds migrate, but a few attempt to overwinter, even in the more northerly part of their range.

CONSERVATION CONCERNS
Species status overall in North America is secure and stable.

Ongoing loss of its marsh habitat, however, may have an effect on future populations.

RELATED SPECIES
Closest relatives are the song sparrow and the Lincoln's sparrow.

The swamp sparrow uses last year's cattail down as lining for its nest

BOBOLINK

Dolichonyx oryzivorus

A male bobolink in breeding plumage

Nothing is more charming than the bubbling, sweet song of a male bobolink as it hovers over a wet meadow in the summertime.

APPEARANCE

Length 7 inches. Wingspan 11 inches. Male and female are distinctly different. The male in breeding plumage has black undersides and is the only North American land bird that is dark below and light above. Upperparts are distinguished by large white patches on the "shoulders" and a white rump. The back of the head and the nape of the neck are buff-colored and the bill is black. The female looks like a large sparrow. It is buff-colored overall with black streaking on the back, sides and rump.

HABITAT

Breeds in open areas such as prairies, fields and wet meadows. Soon after breeding season is over, it congregates in marshes and other wetland areas for a few weeks where it molts its feathers. Winters in the vast grasslands and wetlands of central South America.

The range of the bobolink

BEHAVIOR

Is a gregarious species found in pairs or loose small flocks during the breeding season. They gather into very large flocks before migrating. Forages by gleaning insects and seeds from the grass. The most spectacular behavior is the male's courtship and territorial display in which he suspends himself on vibrating wings while singing.

CALLS

The bobolink has a variety of sounds, the most distinctive being the male's territorial song. Quite unlike the song of any other North American bird. No amount of words can adequately describe it, but the bird's name, in part, comes as close as any: *bobolink-bobolink-bobolink-pink-pink-pink* as an ascending series of bubbling, fluted notes with a metallic overtone. Other calls include a characteristic single *pink* note heard most often in late summer.

A female bobolink

FOOD
Insects, spiders and other invertebrates, seeds of grass and other plants.

FAMILY LIFE
Nest is built on the ground by the female. Materials used include grass and weed stalks, with a lining of fine grasses. Generally five or six eggs are incubated by the female for 10 to 13 days. Both parents tend the young for 10 to 14 days until their first flight. One brood per year.

MIGRATION
Arrives on the breeding grounds in March to early May and leaves on its fall migration between August and October. The bobolink is a neotropical migrant that winters only on the grasslands and wetlands of central South America. It undertakes one of the longest migrations of any North American songbird with a round trip of about 12,000 miles.

CONSERVATION CONCERNS
Species status overall in North America is secure, but there has been a significant population decrease over the past decade. The bobolink is threatened. Over the past few decades its numbers have declined dramatically and its range has contracted. Loss of habitat and the mowing of the hayfields often used for nesting are important causes of the decline. An even more serious concern is the loss of its wintering habitat in Brazil and Paraguay due to the conversion of grassland habitat to agriculture, and the destruction of wetlands by hydroelectric development.

A conservation status map of the bobolink

RELATED SPECIES
The bobolink's closest relatives are blackbirds, grackles and orioles, all of which belong to the *Icteridae* family.

RED-WINGED BLACKBIRD

Ageliaus phoenicius

Red-winged blackbirds perch on cattails where they establish and maintain territories using their familiar konk-a-ree *song*

The red-winged blackbird is an eagerly awaited harbinger of spring. The male's familiar *konk-a-ree, konk-a-ree* song heralds the advance guard of returning migrant birds.

APPEARANCE
Length 7–9 inches. Wingspan 13 inches. It is the size of a robin. Males are larger than females and are a solid, shiny black with distinguishing bright red shoulder epaulets on the front of each wing. Females are streaky brown and gray and look like large sparrows.

HABITAT
Breeding grounds are freshwater marshes, as well as the shallow edges of lakes, ponds and rivers where heavy vegetation such as cattails, bulrushes and reed-grasses grow. Also forages on stubble

The range of the red-winged blackbird

fields, plowed land and other open areas during nonbreeding season.

BEHAVIOR

The male seems to effervesce with energy. While the females are secretive and stay around the immediate area of the nest, males are one of the most conspicuous animals in the marsh. It is often seen perched on a cattail or a reed, flashing its scarlet epaulets while singing. Also does a spectacular song flight where it displays its badges, sings and points its head down in flight from perch to perch. This establishes ownership of a territory when another male intrudes.

Chases off birds much larger than itself that dare to enter its territory such as crows, ravens, northern harriers and other species.

CALLS

Is one of the most vocal residents of a marsh. The male's repertoire includes the *konk-a-ree* song used in territorial displays and

The red-winged blackbird will often scramble among the cattails, sometimes getting into awkward positions

the *cheeert* alarm, a clear descending whistle usually used when a threatening bird such as a hawk, crow or raven appears. Males and females also give a clipped *check* call when alarmed.

FOOD

Outside the breeding season, up to 90 percent of the food eaten are the seeds of grasses and forbs.

During the breeding season, insects make up a large percentage of its diet. The young are fed a diet of 100 percent insects.

FAMILY LIFE
The female builds a cup-shaped nest of loosely woven grasses among cattails or reeds. Three or four eggs are laid and incubated by the female for 10 to 12 days. Young are fed by both parents before leaving the nest after 11 to 14 days. Two or three broods per season.

MIGRATION
Are among the first birds to arrive on more northerly breeding grounds in early March to mid-May. Males arrive first, with females and immature birds following a few weeks later. Fall migration occurs in late September or October.

CONSERVATION CONCERNS
Species status overall in North America is secure and stable. The red-winged blackbird is considered to be one of the most abundant land birds on the continent.

RELATED SPECIES
The red-winged blackbird's closest relative is the very similar tri-colored blackbird of the western United States. Both belong to the genus *Agelaius*.

Did You Know?
Nearly all birds will move or strike poses in a way that communicates something to others of their species. There are visual displays for aggression, courtship, begging, greeting and other purposes, each type meaning a different thing to the intended recipient. A perfect example of this is the territorial display of the male red-winged blackbird. A male red-wing will perform a flight display where it flares its wings to display bright red "badges" to warn intruding males off its territory. This is an example of an aggression display.

COMMON GRACKLE

Quiscalus quiscula

Although appearing black from a distance, a common grackle's plumage is an iridescent blue-green and bronze

Although considered an agricultural pest in many places, this striking and gregarious bird adds an interesting element to the wetland environment.

APPEARANCE

Length 13 inches. Wingspan 17 inches. It is a large, slender and dark bird. Males are a very dark bronze (almost black) with variable muted iridescent colors and a strongly iridescent dark purple head that can be spectacular in the right light. Females are similar, but considerably duller. Both sexes have yellow eyes, long bills and a very long wedge-shaped tail that is keel-shaped in flight. Has relatively long legs.

HABITAT

Open areas such as shorelines, marshes, agricultural areas, wet alder or willow woodlands wet woodlands. Is often seen in cattail marshes.

BEHAVIOR

Outside of the nesting season, the common grackle is very gregarious and can be seen in very

The range of the common grackle

large flocks of hundreds of birds where they often mix with other species such as red-winged blackbirds. Roosts in large flocks at night in trees. Primarily a ground forager in farm fields and other grassy areas. Grackles are also found in cattail and reed marshes where they feed on small aquatic animals and insects. From time to time they wade through the shallow water. They also raid the nests of marsh nesting birds to steal eggs and nestlings.

CALLS

The male's song is a short, rather discordant series of squeaks, sounding much like a rusty screen door opening. Call is a husky sounding *chek*.

FOOD

Diet includes insects, aquatic insects, spiders, fish, eggs, young birds, seeds, grains and acorns.

FAMILY LIFE

Frequently nests in colonies and often near water. Cup-shaped nest is built of grass, twigs, rushes, stems and mud by the female. Is usually placed in trees, occasionally in tree cavities, but also in bushes, shrubs and emergent marsh vegetation such as cattails. Four to six eggs are incubated by the female for 13 or 14 days. Both parents tend the young for 16 to 20 days before they become fledglings. One or two broods per year.

MIGRATION
Is migratory in the northern half of its range. Generally arrives on breeding grounds in mid-February to April. Fall migration occurs during August to December. Birds in the northerly part of the range are overwintering more frequently.

CONSERVATION CONCERNS
Species status overall in North America is secure. Although extremely abundant to the point of becoming a pest in many parts of its range, its numbers may be declining.

RELATED SPECIES
Sister species in North America are the boat-tailed grackle and the great-tailed grackle.

A common grackle eats a red-winged blackbird's egg

WETLAND BIRDS: THE FUTURE

We need the tonic of wildness, to wade sometimes in marshes where the bittern and the meadow-hen lurk, and hear the booming of the snipe; to smell the whispering sedge where only some wilder and more solitary fowl builds her nest, and the mink crawls with its belly close to the ground.

HENRY D. THOREAU

Indeed, humans need the "tonic of wildness," but we are now largely a domesticated species and for most of us, wilderness is just that—a balm to soothe frazzled nerves, a refuge within which we might find solace or spirituality in our manic age, a place to "escape to." Wildness is important for us, but for herons and cranes, geese and ducks, and rails and grebes it is much more. To these and thousands of other species, wilderness isn't a tonic or a concept. It is much more basic, more concrete than that. It is home. It is a place to find food, drink water, rest and reproduce. It has made wetland birds what they are. The shape of their bills, whether they have long or short legs, bright or dull coloration, or make long migrations, etc., are determined in some measure by the way birds have interacted with wetland habitats over thousands of generations. It is as much a part of the animal as the genetic code enfolded in its DNA.

Wetlands are essential for birds and they are disappearing at a rate of about 60 acres per hour. This is an area about the size of sixty football fields lost every hour of every day! These are not merely wastelands being filled in for agriculture and development. For birds, they are places to live.

This ongoing loss of habitat for the continent's birds is tantamount to tearing down our apartment buildings. The people who lived in them must either crowd in with those who live in the buildings that remain (forced crowding is a concept that has never worked in nature or human society), or new buildings must be constructed. Unfortunately, wetlands are being destroyed at a rate that

Red-winged blackbird at daybreak

far outstrips the rate at which they are being created or protected. As a result, bird populations are declining, some of them precipitously. For example, the number of birds crossing the Gulf of Mexico has been cut in half since the 1960s as a result of the loss of wetlands along the coasts of Mississippi and Louisiana. Next door in the Florida Everglades, the situation is also dire.

Fifty years ago Marjory Stoneman Douglas wrote of the Everglades: "They are, they have always been, one of the unique regions of the earth, remote, never wholly known. Nothing anywhere else is like them..." Today they remain largely unknown, still unique and still harboring one of the richest, most complex ecosystems on earth, but they are vanishing and along with them goes wildlife. Half of the Everglades are gone due to agricultural and commercial development and only about 30 percent of the water that once flowed through them still does, and that is polluted.

In Canada and the midwestern United States, up to half of all prairie potholes, wetlands that are vital to 50 percent of the continent's duck population, have been drained for agricultural use. A century ago there were over 3.5 million acres of wintering habitat for snow geese and other wetland species in California's Central Valley. Today there is less than one tenth that. On Canada's East Coast the destruction of wetlands began early. By the late 1700s thousands of acres of prime bird habitat were lost as many of the vast salt marshes around the Bay of Fundy were converted to agricultural lands sequestered behind hundreds of miles of dikes. What impact this may have had on populations of various species isn't known.

There have been successes in protecting and enhancing wetland habitats for birds across North America. The largest effort is sustained under the North American Waterfowl Management Plan. Signed in 1986 by the United States and Canada (Mexico signed on in 1994), its purpose is to restore waterfowl populations by protecting, restoring and enhancing wetland habitat; by doing so it benefits all types of wetland birds. This partnership of federal, state, provincial and local governments, conservation groups, private companies and individuals has invested over $2 billion to protect, restore and enhance more than 7 million acres of wetland habitat. The Ramsar Convention on Wetlands (named after Ramsar, Iran, the birthplace of the convention in 1971) is an international intergovernmental organization whose member countries, including the United States and Canada, agree to follow sustainable practices within "wetlands of international importance." There are fifty-four Ramsar sites in North America. Unfortunately, a number of them have no legal status for the protection of habitat and are sanctuaries in name only. The importance of such large international efforts cannot be argued. However, as critical as these "wetlands of international importance" are, they are only part of the mosaic of wetland habitats found throughout the continent.

Small-scale wetland projects, spearheaded by local communities and groups, often aided by organizations such as Ducks Unlimited, are springing up across the continent. To actually see habitat protected or even created like this is very encouraging. Often they become places to recreate and escape and just enjoy what the natural world has to offer—places that, as Thoreau said, are a "tonic." Over time such familiarity may engender a deeper concern about wetlands and the birds that live in them, resulting in yet more efforts to protect these places and their inhabitants.

A few years ago, in the town that I live in, an old agricultural dike that was meant to hold back the tides was expanded to encircle an unused 35-acre pasture and create an impoundment for holding freshwater. A new marsh was created. Cattails and other marsh plants soon took hold. Within the first year some pioneer red-winged blackbirds, a few black ducks, a pair of Canada geese and some muskrats moved in. Last spring the marsh was a cacophony of spring peeper song. More ducks, foraging great blue herons, nesting pied-billed grebes and tree swallows soon arrived. Cattails colonized its perimeter, creating lots of potential nest sites, cover from predators and shelter from the wind. The frog population exploded and painted turtles could be seen resting in the sun on muskrat houses. It was all beginning to look and sound quite natural.

This past year the little wetland in my town was alive with birds. The familiar ones had returned and were joined by foraging great egrets, a pair of nesting American bitterns and several new species of migrating ducks. In early July, the sky above the marsh was full of swooping swallows and their newly minted young hunting insects. Later that month the first wave of migrating shore-birds arrived, their numbers ultimately swelling into the hundreds by September. Least, semi-palmated, pectoral and white-rumped sandpipers, greater and lesser yellowlegs, dowitchers, snipes, semi-palmated and black-bellied plovers used the marsh to rest and refuel themselves for the long, difficult trip south.

This year something else has happened—more and more people began visiting this once-fallow field, now a genuine working wetland. A trail circling the marsh was completed in the spring, and walkers, joggers and birders began to "flock" to it. Now it is a cherished place to visit for many residents of the town. This little marsh is an example of what can be done when the will to do it exists.

Although we like to think we live in an enlightened environmental age, a time when the tragedy of habitat loss and extinction should be abating, we mustn't fool ourselves. Progress has been made, but depending on the mood of the time, progress can be unmade, too. As the great conservationist Aldo Leopold wrote fifty years ago, "Despite nearly a century of propaganda, conservation

A group of American white pelicans in a lagoon at sunset

still proceeds at a snail's pace; progress still consists largely of letterhead pieties and convention oratory. On the back forty we still slip two steps backwards for each forward stride." The pressure humans bring to bear on the birds of the wetlands will always be there, in one form or another, be it destruction of their habitat, pollution or hunting. Whether or how well they survive in light of this will ultimately depend on how much we decide to care.

Radar is an effective tool for following birds on migration. Showing up as small blips on the radar screen, individuals can be distinguished from flocks, and flight speed can also be estimated. Radar has proven useful in conservation in the past. Multiyear records from radar stations along the Gulf of Mexico coast helped determine that a large decrease in the number of birds migrating over that body of water occurred between the 1960s and 1980s.

SELECTED BIBLIOGRAPHY

Alsop III, Fred J. *Birds of Canada*. Dorling Kindersley Handbooks, 2002.

Armstrong, Edward A. *A Study of Bird Song*. Dover Publications, 1973.

Armstrong, Edward A. *The Ethology of Bird Display and Bird Behavior*, Revised Edition. Dover Publications, 1965.

Askins, Robert A. *Restoring North America's Birds*. Yale University Press, 2000.

Attenborough, David. *The Life of Birds*. BBC Books, 1998.

Audubon, John James. *Audubon's Birds of America*, Popular edition. The MacMillan Company, 1950.

Bent, Arthur Cleveland. *Life Histories of North American Birds of Prey*, Part One. Dover Edition, 1961. (Originally published 1937.)

Bent, Arthur Cleveland. *Life Histories of North American Gulls and Terns*. Dover Edition, 1963. (Originally published 1921.)

Bent, Arthur Cleveland. *Life Histories of North American Marsh Birds*. Dover Edition, 1963. (Originally published 1926.)

Bent, Arthur Cleveland. *Life Histories of North American Shore Birds*, Part One. Dover Edition, 1962. (Originally published 1927.)

Bird, David M. *The Bird Alamanac*. Key Porter Books, 1999.

Borror, Donald J. *Bird Song and Bird Behavior*. Dover Publications, 1972.

Brooke, Michael and Tim Birkhead, eds. *The Cambridge Encyclopedia of Ornithology*. Cambridge University Press, 1991.

Carwardine, Mark. *Birds in Focus*. Salamander Books, 1990.

Chapman, Frank M. *Bird Life*. D. Appleton and Company, 1910.

Douglas, Marjory Stoneman. *The Everglades: River of Grass*. Mockingbird Books, 1947.

Eastman, John. *Birds of Lake, Pond and Marsh*. Stackpole Books, 1999.

Ehrlich, Paul R. *The Machinery of Nature*. Touchstone Books, 1986.

Ehrlich, Paul R., David S. Dobkin and Darryl Wheye. *The Birder's Handbook*. Fireside Books, 1988.

Erskine, Anthony J. *Atlas of Breeding Birds of the Maritime Provinces*. Nimbus/Nova Scotia Museum, 1992.

Feduccia, Alan. *The Origin and Evolution of Birds*, 2nd ed. Yale University Press, 1999.

Fish and Wildlife Service. *Migration of Birds*, Circular 16. U.S. Dept. of the Interior, 1950.

Gill, Frank. *Ornithology*, 2nd ed. W.H. Freeman & Company, 1995.

Godfrey, W. Earl. *The Birds of Canada*, Revised edition. National Museum of Natural Sciences, 1986.

Harrison, Hal H. *Birds' Nests*. Houghton Mifflin Company, 1975.

Heinrich, Bernd. *Racing the Antelope*. Cliff Street Books, 2001.

Jones, John Oliver. *The U.S. Outdoor Atlas & Recreation Guide*. Houghton Mifflin Company, 1992.

Jones, John Oliver. *Where the Birds Are*. Morrow, 1990.

Keddy, Paul. *Wetland Ecology: Principles and Conservation*. Cambridge University Press, 2000.

Leopold, Aldo. *A Sand County Almanac*. Oxford University Press, 1949.

Livingston, John A. *The Fallacy of Wildlife Conservation*. McClelland and Stewart, 1981.

Low, Gary and W. Mansell. *North American Marsh Birds*. Harper & Row, 1983.

Marzluff, John M. and Rex Sallabanks. *Avian Conservation*. Island Press, 1998.

Mitsch, William and James Gosselink. *Wetlands*, 3rd Edition. John Wiley & Sons, 2000.

NatureServe. *NatureServe Explorer: An online encyclopedia of life*, version 4.1. Available at www.natureserve.org/explorer. NatureServe, 2004.

Peattie, Donald Culross. *Flowering Earth*. Compass Books, 1961.

Peterson, Roger Tory. *Eastern Birds*. Houghton Mifflin, 1980.

Poole, A. and F. Gill, eds. *The Birds of North America Life Histories for the 21st Century*. The Birds of North America Inc., 1992.

Pough, Richard H. *Audubon Water Bird Guide*. Doubleday, 1951.

Ridgely, R.S., T.F. Allnut, T. Brooks, D.K. McNicol, D.W. Mehlman, B.E. Young, and J.R. Zook. *Digital Distribution Maps of the Birds of the Western Hemisphere*, version 1.0. NatureServe, 2003.

Robbins, Chandler S., Bertel Bruun, Herbert S. Zim and Arthur Singer. *Birds of North America*, Expanded, Revised Edition. Golden, 1983.

Root, Terry. *Atlas of Wintering North American Birds: An Analysis of Christmas Bird Count Data*. University of Chicago Press, 1998.

Sibley, David Allen. *The Sibley Guide to Birds*. Knopf, 2000.

Sibley, David Allen, John B. Dunning Jr. and Chris Elphick, eds. *The Sibley Guide to Bird Life & Behavior*. Knopf, 2001.

Skutch, Alexander F. *Origins of Nature's Beauty*. The University of Texas Press, 1992.

Stokes, Donald & Lillian. *A Guide to Bird Behavior*, Vols. 1, 2 and 3. Little Brown, 1979, 1983, 1989.

Sutton, Clay and Patricia Taylor Sutton. *How to Spot Hawks and Eagles*. Chapters Publishing, 1996.

Teal, John and Mildred Teal. *The Life and Death of the Salt Marsh*. Ballantine Books, 1969.

Teale, Edwin Way. *Green Treasury*. Dodd, Mead & Company, 1952.

Thoreau, Henry David. *Thoreau on Birds*. Beacon Press, 1910.

Tudge, Colin. *The Variety of Life*. Oxford University Press, 2000.

Tufts, Robie W. *Birds of Nova Scotia*, Third edition. Nimbus Publishing / Nova Scotia Museum, 1986.

Weiner, Jonathan. *The Beak of the Finch*. Vintage Books, 1994.

Weller, Milton W. *Wetland Birds: Habitat Resources and Conservation Implications*. Cambridge University Press, 1999.

Wernert, Susan, ed. *North American Wildlife*. Reader's Digest Association, 1982.

SELECTED IMPORTANT WETLANDS IN CANADA

Below is a selection of important wetland bird areas in Canada. This list is not exhaustive by any means, but is representative of some of the wonderful places that exist for wetland birds in Canada. You can find additional areas by visiting many of the websites listed below, particularly the Canadian Wildlife Service, which administers Canada's migratory bird sanctuaries and national wildlife areas.

VASEUX LAKE MIGRATORY BIRD SANCTUARY,
BRITISH COLUMBIA
Canadian Wildlife Service
5421 Robertson Rd., RR #1
Delta, BC V4K 3N2
website: www.pyr.ec.gc.ca/en/wildlife/index.shtml

Nearly 700 acres comprise the shallow Vaseux Lake, which is an important migratory area for trumpeter swans, as well as dabbling duck species, American coots and grebes. It is contiguous with Vaseux-Bighorn National Wildlife Area, which is home to a population of California bighorn sheep—rare in Canada.

COLUMBIA NATIONAL WILDLIFE AREA, BRITISH COLUMBIA
Canadian Wildlife Service
5421 Robertson Rd., RR #1
Delta, BC V4K 3N2
website: www.pyr.ec.gc.ca/en/wildlife/index.shtml

Approximately 2,500 acres comprised of four separate river-bottom wetland areas along the Columbia River are an important migratory stopover for many species of waterfowl including tundra swans, trumpeter swans, Canada geese, mallards, American wigeons and other species. It is also an important nesting habitat for cavity-nesting ducks such as buffleheads, wood ducks and hooded mergansers.

GEORGE C. REIFEL MIGRATORY BIRD SANCTUARY,
BRITISH COLUMBIA
Canadian Wildlife Service
5421 Robertson Rd., RR #1
Delta, BC V4K 3N2
website: www.pyr.ec.gc.ca/en/wildlife/index.shtml

Comprises 1,600 acres of tidal marsh, mudflats, freshwater marsh and grassy areas located at the northern end of Westham Island in the mouth of the Fraser River, this is an important sanctuary for migratory shorebirds and waterfowl, including 25,000 lesser snow geese. Wintering birds include thousands of dabbling and diving ducks such as mallards, wigeon, teals, buffleheads and mergansers. Great blue herons can be observed during winter hunting rodents in dry upland areas.

BEAVERHILL LAKE, ALBERTA
Fish & Wildlife Services
South Tower, Petroleum Plaza
9915–108th St.
Edmonton, AB T5K 2G6
website: www.mb.ec.gc.ca/nature

About 45,000 acres of Beaverhill Lake and surrounding habitats located at the edge of the aspen parkland zone in central Alberta, provide vital habitat for 200,000 ducks, geese, and swans during their spring and fall migration.

PEACE-ATHABASKA DELTA, ALBERTA
Superintendent
Wood Buffalo National Park
P.O. Box 750
Fort Smith, NWT XOE OPO
website: www.mb.ec.gc.ca/nature

At almost 1 million acres, this is the largest boreal delta in the world, one of the most important waterfowl nesting and staging areas on the continent, a staging area for waterfowl migrating to the MacKenzie River lowlands, Arctic deltas and Arctic islands. More than a million birds use the delta during the fall.

HAY-ZAMA WILDLAND PROVINCIAL PARK, ALBERTA
Fish & Wildlife Services
South Tower, Petroleum Plaza
9915–108 St.
Edmonton, AB T5K 2G8
website: www.mb.ec.gc.ca/nature

The park is approximately 120,000 acres of lakes, floodplains and interior deltas located in northwestern Alberta. Up to 375,000 migratory waterfowl from three flyways (Pacific, central and Mississippi) congregate here and use the area during the fall.

LAST MOUNTAIN LAKE NATIONAL WILDLIFE AREA, SASKATCHEWAN
Canadian Wildlife Service
Twin Atrium Building, Room 200
4999–98th Ave.
Edmonton, AB T6B 2X3
website: www.prn-rpn.ec.ca/nature

Over 38,000 acres in southern Saskatchewan of which 21 percent is extremely productive wetlands, including wet meadows, prairie potholes, marshes, salty mudflats and the lake itself, these rare native prairie grasslands cover one half of the national wildlife area. Over 280 species of birds have been observed here. Up to 50,000 cranes, almost half a million geese and several hundred thousand ducks rely on the area during peak migration.

QUILL LAKES SASKATCHEWAN RAMSAR SITE,
SASKATCHEWAN
Fish & Wildlife Services
3211 Albert St.
Regina, SK S4S 5W6
website: www.mb.ec.gc.ca/nature

About 44,000 acres comprising three wetlands, the Big Quill, Middle Quill and Little Quill lakes provide a key breeding area for waterfowl and other waterbirds. This is an important stopover for 155,000 migrating shorebirds. A potash mine has been approved for the development on Big Quill Lake. The threat to endangered piping plovers that utilize the lake could be considerable.

DELTA MARSH, MANITOBA
Wildlife Branch
P.O. Box 24, 200 Saulteaux Cres.
Winnipeg, MB R3J 3W3
website: www.mb.ec.gc.ca/nature

Over 40,000 acres of large freshwater marshes and small sloughs adjacent to Lake Manitoba in southern Manitoba are a key migratory staging area for an average of 50,000 dabbling ducks during the fall.

OAK HAMMOCK MARSH WILDLIFE MANAGEMENT AREA,
MANITOBA
Manitoba Conservation
P.O. Box 24, 200 Saulteaux Cres.
Winnipeg, MB R3J 3W3
website: www.ducks.ca

Nearly 9,000 acres, including four man-made freshwater marsh impoundments and fifty-eight nesting islands, comprise one of the most important waterfowl staging and migratory areas on the prairies of western Canada with over 400,000 ducks and geese present at peak migration. A large interpretation center and the national headquarters of Ducks Unlimited Canada are on site.

POINT PELEE NATIONAL PARK, ONTARIO
407 Monarch Lane, RR #1
Leamington, ON N8H 3V4
website: www.pc.gc.ca/pn-np/on/pelee/index_e.asp

Over 3,800 acres of marsh, swamp and Carolinian forest cover the southernmost part of a peninsula in Lake Erie, Canada's most southerly point. This is one of the most renowned migration spots in North America. Over 360 species have been observed here during migration, including an abundance of waterfowl, shorebirds and songbirds.

WYE MARSH WILDLIFE MANAGEMENT AREA, ONTARIO
16160 Hwy 12, P.O. Box 100
Midland, ON L4R 4K6
website: www.wyemarsh.com

Over 2,200 acres of cattail freshwater marsh, small fens and shallow open water provide key nesting habitat for many wetland species including a number of uncommon species such as black terns, least bitterns and trumpeter swans.

SOUTHERN JAMES BAY MIGRATORY BIRD SANCTUARIES, ONTARIO
Ontario Ministry of Natural Resources
2 Third Street
Cochrane, ON P0L 1C0
website: www.collections.ic.gc.ca/sanctuaries/nwt/akimi.htm

Approximately 66,000 acres of tidal marshes, mudflats and eel-grass beds, located in two sanctuaries (Hannah Bay and Moose River) in the southern end of James Bay in northern Ontario. This is one of the most important staging areas in northern North America for migratory and breeding Arctic wetland birds. Thousands of ducks, shorebirds and up to 150,000 snow geese use the area.

CAP TOURMENTE NATIONAL WILDLIFE AREA, QUEBEC
Canadian Wildlife Service
1141 route de l'Eglisse
CP 10100, 9e etage
Sainte-Foy, QC G1V 4H5
website: www.qc.ec.gc.ca/

These 5,500 acres of tidal marsh, artificial waterfowl ponds and coastal marsh provide one of the most important migratory stopovers for the greater snow goose in North America. About 800,000 geese stop here during both spring and fall migrations. Many other species also rely on the area.

SHEPODY BAY NATIONAL WILDLIFE AREA, NEW BRUNSWICK
Canadian Wildlife Service
P.O. Box 6227, Sackville, NB E4L 1G6
website: www.atl.ec.gc.ca/wildlife

Approximately 2,400 acres of fresh and saltwater marsh and tidal mudflats on the Upper Bay of Fundy, along with Nova Scotia's Evangeline Beach across the bay (which is currently not protected), the Mary's Point section of the Shepody National Wildlife Area is the most important fall migration stop on the continent for the semi-palmated sandpiper with up to 1 million of these birds present at peak migration. Other parts of the area are important migration staging areas for waterfowl.

CHIGNECTO NATIONAL WILDLIFE AREA, NOVA SCOTIA
Canadian Wildlife Service
P.O. Box 6227
Sackville, NB E4L 1G6
website: www.atl.ec.gc.ca/wildlife

This comprises over 2,500 acres of salt marsh, freshwater marsh impoundments, bogs, ponds and upland areas. Salt marsh areas are key migratory stopover and staging areas for ducks and geese. Part of the national wildlife area, Amherst Point Migratory Bird Sanctuary boasts some of the highest waterfowl and marsh bird productivity in Atlantic Canada.

MALPEQUE BAY, PRINCE EDWARD ISLAND
Canadian Wildlife Service
P.O. Box 6227
Sackville, NB E4L 1G6
website: www.atl.ec.gc.ca/widlife

Approximately 23,000 acres are comprised largely of shallow estuary waters and mudflats, as well as salt marsh, salt ponds, sand dunes and beach. Up to 20,000 Canada geese, 3,000 red-breasted mergansers and 1,500 American black ducks, among others, use the estuary and surrounding areas during migration. Shorebirds are abundant during fall migration and several pairs of endangered piping plovers nest here. The largest great blue heron colony in Prince Edward Island is found on an island in the bay.

GRAND CODROY ESTUARY,
NEWFOUNDLAND AND LABRADOR
Canadian Wildlife Service
P.O. Box 6227
Sackville, NB E4L 1G6
website: www.atl.ec.gc.ca/widlife

Over 5,000 acres are made up largely of shallow, brackish wetlands and mudflats, with a lesser area comprised of a meandering shallow estuarine river channel. Eelgrass is abundant in areas. This is an important staging area for up to 20,000 Canada geese and American black ducks as well an important area for the endangered piping plover.

SELECTED IMPORTANT
WETLANDS IN THE
UNITED STATES

Below is a selection of important wetland bird areas in the United States. This list is not exhaustive by any means, but is meant to be representative of some of the wonderful places for wetland birds in America. You can find additional areas by visiting many of the websites listed below, particularly the U.S. Fish and Wildlife Service, which administers the national wildlife refuge system.

DON EDWARDS SAN FRANCISCO BAY NATIONAL WILDLIFE REFUGE
P.O. Box 524
Newark, CA 94560
website: http://desfbay.fws.gov

Millions of shorebirds and waterfowl stop here during spring and fall migration on 30,000 acres of open bay, salt ponds, salt marsh, mudflats, upland and vernal pools located throughout the southern part of San Francisco Bay.

KLAMATH BASIN NATIONAL WILDLIFE REFUGES COMPLEX
4009 Hill Road
Tulelake, CA 96134
website: http://klamathbasinrefuges.fws.gov/index.html

Six national wildlife refuges, totaling over 192,000 acres of largely wetlands and open water, are located in northern California/southern Oregon. A peak of nearly 1 million waterfowl use the refuges during fall migration and the largest congregation of bald eagles in the lower forty-eight states—at 500 birds—spends the winter here.

BEAR RIVER NATIONAL WILDLIFE REFUGE
58 South 950 West
Brigham City, UT 84302
website: http://bearriver.fws.gov

The 74,000 acres of marsh, open water and mudflats along with uplands, wet meadows and ponds around the Green, Cuchense and White rivers are a critical migratory stopover for shorebirds and waterfowl, including 30,000 tundra swans in the fall. It is also an important wintering area for raptors such as northern harriers, rough-legged hawks, prairie falcons and bald eagles.

BOSQUE DEL APACHE NATIONAL WILDLIFE REFUGE
P.O. Box 1246
Socorro, NM 87801
website: http://southwest.fws.gov/refuges/newmex/bosque.html

Located at the northern edge of the Chihuahuan Desert, 57,191 acres along the Rio Grande River, comprised of moist bottomlands, floodplains and other wilderness, are a refuge for over 340 species of birds, including 30,000 snow geese, 12,000 sandhill cranes and 20,000 ducks during winter. Endangered whooping cranes may be found during winter as well.

DES LACS NATIONAL WILDLIFE REFUGE
P.O. Box 578
Kenmare, ND 58746
website: http://deslacs.fws.gov/deslacs.html

Lakes and managed wetlands on 19,500 acres along the Des Lacs River in North Dakota, near the Canadian border, provide a critical area for migrating and nesting waterfowl and marsh birds, including hundreds of thousands of lesser snow geese and tundra swans every fall.

CHEYENNE BOTTOMS WILDLIFE AREA
c/o Great Bend Visitors Bureau
P.O. Box 274
Great Bend, KS 67530
website: www.cheyennebottoms.net

Freshwater wetlands on 41,000 acres of which 19,857 are managed by the state of Kansas and 7,300 by the Nature Conservancy, are one of the most important shorebird migratory stopovers in North America. It is used by thirty-nine species of shorebirds during spring, summer and fall with as many as 600,000 birds present in the fall.

ARANSAS NATIONAL WILDLIFE REFUGE
P.O. Box 100
Austwell, TX 77950
website: http://southwest.fws.gov/refuges/texas/aransas.html

The refuge's 70,504 acres of uplands, grasslands and surrounding tidal marshes provide a home for cranes, including the endangered whooping crane. Wintering herons, egrets, spoonbills, shorebirds and waterfowl are also found here.

LAGUNA ATASCOSA NATIONAL WILDLIFE REFUGE
P.O. Box 450
Rio Hondo, TX 78583
website: http://southwest.fws.gov/refuges/texas/laguna.html

As the southernmost waterfowl refuge in the U.S. and at 45,000 acres, this is the largest protected area in the Lower Rio Grande Valley. It is home to endangered or threatened species such as wood stork, piping plover and the bald eagle. During winter it is a key area for waterfowl, particularly redhead—most of its North American population winters here. Many species of long-legged waders are also found here.

MERRITT ISLAND NATIONAL WILDLIFE REFUGE
P.O. Box 6504
Titusville, FL 32782
website: www.merrittisland.fws.gov

Approximately 140,000 acres of mostly brackish marshes and salt
marshes on Merritt Island on the central east coast of Florida are
adjacent to the Kennedy Space Center and Cape Canaveral
National Seashore. Over 500 species of wildlife, including tens of
thousands of ducks and other migratory wetland birds stop there
during the winter. It is one of the best places in the world to photograph wetland birds.

CHAUTAUQUA NATIONAL WILDLIFE REFUGE
19031 E. Country Road 2110N
Havana, IL 62644
website: http://midwest.fws.gov/chautauqua.html

About 6,200 acres along the Illinois River, located on the
Mississippi flyway are a vital resting and feeding area for migratory
waterfowl and other birds. Up to 250,000 waterfowl and 10,000
shorebirds depend on the refuge.

SABINE NATIONAL WILDLIFE REFUGE
3000 Holly Beach Highway
Hackberry, LA 70645
website: http://sabine.fws.gov

The 124,000 acres of marshes between Calcasieu and Sabine lakes
in southwestern Louisiana are an important overwintering area for
waterfowl, including very large flocks of snow geese. It is also an
important migratory stopover for shorebirds.

SWAN LAKE NATIONAL WILDLIFE REFUGE
Rt. 1, Box 29A
Sumner, MO 64681
website: http://midwest.fws.gov/swanlake.html

The 10,795 acres of wetlands near the confluence of the Grand and Missouri rivers are an important nesting, feeding and resting area for waterfowl. Between 10,000 and 80,000 Canada geese use the reserve annually.

EVERGLADES NATIONAL PARK
40001 State Road 9336
Homestead, FL 330304–6733
website: www.nps.gov/ever/

This is the only subtropical wilderness preserve in North America. The 1,508,537 acres, largely wetlands, span southern Florida. There is extremely rich bird life, with a total population in the millions. It has been designated as a Wetland of International Importance, a World Heritage Site and an International Biosphere Reserve.

BOMBAY HOOK NATIONAL WILDLIFE REFUGE
2591 Whitehall Neck Road
Smyrna, DE 19977
website: http://bombayhook.fws.gov

These 15,978 acres are mostly salt marsh, some of the largest tidal salt marshes left in the mid-Atlantic. It is extremely important area for the protection and conservation of waterfowl, particularly in the fall.

CAPE MAY NATIONAL WILDLIFE REFUGE
24 Kimbles Beach Rd.
Cape May Court House
Cape May, NJ 08210–2078
website: http://capemay.fws.gov

Over 110,000 acres are a vital coastal and salt marsh habitat for hundreds of thousands of migratory birds on the Atlantic flyway migration route. The 317 bird species, including twenty species of shorebirds, depend on Cape May. Virtually the entire North

American population of red knots gather here and on surrounding beaches during the spring migration. The area is also known for its spectacular display of hawk migrations in the fall.

CHINCOTEAGUE NATIONAL WILDLIFE REFUGE
P.O. Box 62
Chincoteague Island, VA 23336
website: http://chinco.fws.gov

Over 14,000 acres of beach, marsh, dunes and forest, mostly located on Assateague Island, provide an important habitat for tens of thousands of migratory shorebirds, wading birds, waterfowl (up to 50,000 snow geese) and songbirds. It is one of the top five migratory sites for shorebirds east of the Rockies.

WETLAND BIRDS
INTERNET RESOURCES

Here are names and website addresses for a selection of organizations involved in bird conservation and birding in North America. All of these are great organizations that do critical, commendable work and all of them deserve our support. Some of the websites, especially NatureServe, BirdSource and the Cornell Laboratory of Ornithology, are also great learning resources that offer an astonishing amount of information about birds' natural history and their conservation.

AMERICAN BIRDING ASSOCIATION
www.americanbirding.org

BIRDLIFE INTERNATIONAL
www.birdlife.net

BIRDSOURCE
www.birdsource.org

BIRD STUDIES CANADA
www.bsc-eoc.org

CANADIAN NATURE FEDERATION
www.cnf.ca/bird

CORNELL LABORATORY OF ORNITHOLOGY
www.birds.cornell.edu

DUCKS UNLIMITED CANADA
www.ducks.ca

DUCKS UNLIMITED U.S.A.
www.ducks.org

NATIONAL AUDUBON SOCIETY
www.audubon.org

PARTNERS IN FLIGHT
www.partnersinflight.org

NATURESERVE
www.natureserve.org

ACKNOWLEDGEMENTS

Thanks to Paula Leslie, whose keen eye and constructive criticism, among other things, have been a huge contribution to this book.

Thanks to the authors of scores of field guides over the past century who have laid the foundation of natural history knowledge for the rest of us to enjoy and build upon. Like so many who write about the lives of North American birds, I owe a particular debt of gratitude to the work of Arthur Cleveland Bent and his many volume set on the life histories of North American birds, first published more than six decades ago.

Thanks to the millions of birders all over the continent whose passion and enthusiasm for the natural world have become a force for protecting it.

Thanks to NatureServe for generously giving permission to use its western hemisphere range maps and distribution maps. Range map data was provided by NatureServe in collaboration with Robert Ridgely, James Zook, The Nature Conservancy-Migratory Bird Program, Conservation International–CABS, World Wildlife Fund-US and Environment Canada–WILDSPACE.

A special thanks to Leo MacDonald for his instrumental efforts in helping to make this book possible.

Thanks to Michael Mouland and the staff at Key Porter Books for their friendly professionalism, expertise and faith in this project. Thanks to Heather and Ken Roberts for their support.

My deepest gratitude to my father, Lloyd "Jack" Leslie, who has always encouraged me to follow my own path in life and has taught me that just about anything is possible.

Thank you to Jean Leslie for her wonderful encouragment and support.

Last but not least, I give thanks to the birds themselves, and all the other non-human beings sharing the Earth with us, without whose kinds this glorious planet would be a barren, monotonous place. Among them are two particular four-legged friends, Buddy and Heikki.

INDEX